Go!
You Are Sent

Genie Summers

Charleston Press, Inc.
Baton Rouge, Louisiana

Copyright © 1995, all rights reserved
by Genie Summers

No part of this book may be reproduced in any form or by any means without the express written consent of the author. Brief passages may be quoted without permission in the body of reviews for the limited purpose of reviewing this book. For more information, contact the publisher.

Library of Congress Catalog Card Number 95-83061

ISBN 0-935773-57-6

Published by Charleston Press, Inc.
4911 S. Sherwood Forest Blvd.
Baton Rouge, Louisiana 70816
(504) 293-9472

Printed in the United States
Cover design by Lunar Graphics, Inc.

Foreword

I first met Frank and Genie Summers and their family, "by chance," in the airport on Fiji in the South Pacific. I was inspired to meet this family who at that time were lay missionaries on the Tonga Islands. Since then I have been privileged to keep in touch with their work as they continued to serve in various regions in the South Pacific, then in the Philippines, in Mexico, and now back in the United States.

Over the years both my wife and I have been encouraged and inspired to keep on serving the Lord ourselves as we have seen the life and work of the Summers family unfold. Now we are thrilled that this remarkable story has been put into book form and will be available to many others.

Even if we never leave home, all of us are called to be servants of the Lord where we are planted, and this book will be an inspiration and help to all in following the Lord whatever the circumstances.

Ralph Martin

Author's Note: Ralph Martin was the founding editor of *New Covenant* magazine. His books, *A Crisis of Truth*, *Hungry for God*, and *The Catholic Church at the end of an Age: What is the Spirit Saying?* have shaped the renewal movement in the Catholic Church. He heads up Renewal Ministries and co-hosts *The Choices We Face*, a talk show on EWTN. His Speaking ministry on evangelism, renewal and the mission of the church covers both the national and international circuit.

Acknowledgments

Only God can repay everyone who had a part in the writing of this book. At the risk of leaving out scores of encouraging friends, I want to thank Carlos and Lenny in General Cepeda, Mexico, who loaned me their summer home for the writing of the first draft; Mickey Little, Betty Dore, Cheryl Romero, and Florence Crain who typed the second draft; Paul Patout, Pat Miller and the Guillory family who donated computers or computer time. Valerie Marko "held down the fort" for a week, while I wrote. I leaned heavily on Cheryl and Donald Romero for support and the care of my boys. Hundreds of our prayer partners stormed heaven. Shawn Gardiner precipitated the final publishing effort. Dr. David Thibodeaux's corrections were invaluable. The Writer's Guild of Acadiana helped me understand the needs of today's readers. Mom and Dad were first to teach me about God, and to love writing. Beau's enthusiastic promotion of *Go* in its final form was essential. I am most indebted to my family, Frank and the children, who lived our adventure and patiently endured the time I gave to this book.

A final thanks goes to all who have heard and believed the Good News that we proclaimed. They made our story possible.

To Frank,
Who lays down his life for me

Genie Summers, wife, mother and foreign Lay Catholic Missionary Evangelist, has been published seriously since the early 1970's. She was the Lifestyles Editor of the Abbeville Meridional, published and directed a documentary film, a play about her Cajun grandmother, and wrote editorials and articles in both the Christian and secular press. Most recently she was the founding editor of the Caroline Catholic, published by the Diocese of the Caroline Islands in the Federated States of Micronesia. This is her first book length work. Her family's life and work have appeared in the printed media, on television and radio, and been heartily endorsed by the bishops of the dioceses where they serve.

Also I heard the voice of the Lord, saying, whom shall I send, and who will go for us? Then said I, Here am I; send me.

Isaiah 6:8

Chapter One

A Place of Beginnings

The movement of the Spanish moss dangling from the Kisinoak trees held me in a moment of nostalgia. The sniffling of my little sister, and the earthy aroma of freshly cut St. Augustine grass filled the air. "Here I go!" I managed to say.

Assessing the weight of this event, I asked myself, "I'm off to college, moving out. Am I ready for this?" Doubts darted past my determination, "Did I cross an imaginary bridge? It all went by so fast."

Daddy pulled up to the oaks that had reached out to each other in a kiss. I was sore from hugs, and tears had stained my starched khaki shorts. My ten year old brother, Brian, huffed and puffed, leaning to the side like a waterlogged pine in a hurricane, carrying my new luggage to the car.

Beginnings were ending. Endings were beginning. I knew it. The day I left home for Louisiana State University in June of 1961 was not an ordinary day.

My baby sister, Rachel, was standing like a little beacon of brightness beneath the twenty foot columns of the front porch. She called out bravely, "You better come back before I grow up."

"You can wait 'til I grow up," Bruce shouted through a sneaky smile. "Then I can have your car!"

I slammed the trunk shut, and with both hands free, blew kisses madly at the kids and Mommee, my pretty, petite, Cajun grandmother. As we pulled out of the driveway, something

Go! You Are Sent

significant stayed behind at "Kisinoaks." I was the oldest of five, and the first to leave the nest. There would never be quite the same togetherness again.

My parents' home on ten acres is called "Kisinoaks." The antebellum house sits on one of loveliest spots in Abbeville. Rachel and the boys loved the hiding places and secret passageways. Most of the windows opened onto a view of the bends in the bayou. Several acres of woods run the length of the other side.

"I'm excited," I sobbed, "I really do want to go, but I hate to leave. I'd hate to think of what it would have been like if I had gone to that woman's college in Virginia. At least LSU is only a couple of hours away. I can bring my car up in the fall, can't I?"

"That's what I understand. You can have your car in the fall. Get used to the campus first. If you had your car now, you'd never absorb the atmosphere. And, if I know you, you'd be headed home too soon," Mama said.

Transplanting a Cajun is not easy. LSU held an allure for me, but the epic emotion I felt as the motor purred and Daddy shifted into drive was the ordeal of leaving loved ones. Our T-Bird sat down low, extra loaded with my college gear. I climbed into the back seat, slipped off my sandals and arranged my things that hadn't fit into the trunk. We reached the main road. Shrubbery was about to block out the last view of Kisinoaks.

I glanced back up at my own "Southern Belle" balcony. My room opened onto a balcony that looked out on the columns of the front porch. I often curled up on there with a good book and watched the bayou mosey along. When I daydreamed of my wedding day, as all seventeen year old girls do, I dreamed of throwing my bridal bouquet from that romantic spot.

"Mom, you're not going to let the boys sleep in my room all the time, are you? They do that because they say making one bed is faster than making three!"

"Don't worry," she assured me. "I've warned them. Your room is your room. Maybe, one day when you get married, Rachel will move up there. I hope she'll have her leg braces off by then."

Rachel was born with Spina-Bifida (a birth defect involving an open spinal column). At fourteen, I had waited through the birth of four brothers for a baby sister. They gave her a fifty-fifty chance of survival at birth. During my high school years, we had been a twosome. I usually swooped her up, her leg braces clanging like bells, and off we went in my little shrimp colored foreign car to run errands or visit friends.

"I'm going to miss Rachel so much, I'm coming home for her fourth birthday no matter what. I'll miss school if I have to," I told my parents as we drove into Lafayette, the next bayou town along the way.

"Look, Genie, coming to summer school was your idea. You could have waited 'til the fall," Daddy said, reminding me of my decision.

"Becoming a doctor takes a long time. I wanted to get started right away," I explained.

"Well, you can't study medicine in Abbeville, give it a couple of weeks and we'll probably have to beg you to come back to Kisinoaks."

Among the things that I had taken special care to keep with me in the back seat of the car was a picture frame. In preparation for leaving home, I had painstakingly made up a collage of family photos. I had put in a photo, processed a memory, put in another photo, processed another memory, until I had a full frame and a full heart. The collage contained a deliberate reconstruction of the good life at home. All the dark spots had been edited out.

Our family was really close knit, but that's how families were in my home town of Abbeville. I felt like leaving Abbeville was not something anyone should ever do without ceremoniously marking the occasion. My collage of family photographs was for me that historic marker.

The "laughing" picture that giggled at me from the upper left hand corner was the first I had placed there. Mommee had taken it, and captured all of us in a hearty burst of laughter. The Gremillions are an impulsive, passionate bunch. Our Cajun blood beats to the rhythm of the good times. Our good times were super-charged. But the tragedy is that our bad times were fuel injected. More often than not, that fuel was one hundred proof. Alcoholism lurked around us like a stealthy predator, waiting to ravage every happy occasion. How I hated that archenemy of our family. And yet, I was already learning to drink with the best of them. I believed in the "let the good times roll" motto of Cajun country.

One photo I had placed in my frame was of my little brother Robin. I was thirteen when he was born, old enough to give him his bottle, change him, and rock him. One night, my friend Judy called on the telephone, "Are you going to the movies tonight? We can give you a ride."

"I was planning to go, but Mama and Daddy are going out. I think I'll stay home and help 'Sweet Sue' (our wonderful babysitter) take care of the baby," I said.

"You can play with him all day tomorrow. Why don't you come? *Everybody* is going to be there!" she pushed a little.

Normally, I would have been convinced. Friday night movies were the highlight of the week for kids in Abbeville, and I rarely missed one. This night was different. I couldn't explain my determination to stay with the baby.

"Okay, 'Little Mama,' you can dress the baby in his pajamas and give him his bottle," Sweet Sue told me as she shuffled down the hall to put my other little brothers to sleep.

"You better drink all of your milk, cutie pie. It's good and warm," I told him. That night, I fed and cuddled him. I let him wrap his little fingers around my index finger. He gave me a big smile after he burped. I held him until he fell asleep and then I put him in his crib. When my parents came home later, the baby was asleep.

Early morning at our house followed a routine. Daddy was always the early riser. First, he'd make the coffee and heat the baby's bottle. Then he would awaken Mama to change and feed the baby. Together they read the paper and got the rest of us up for the day.

The morning after I stayed home from the movies I was shocked into consciousness by the screams of my father, "Beverlee, Beverlee, our baby's dead!"

I was frozen, hoping it was a bad dream, but then I could hear Mama screaming, "Oh no, oh no!!"

I ran into their bedroom. There was Mama with Robin cradled in her arms; she looked up at me and said, "Bring me some blankets, he's so cold, he's so cold."

I ran into the other room with the tightest knot imaginable in my throat. In my heart I was crying out, "God help us!" In my mind, somehow, I knew the blankets wouldn't help.

Not knowing what else to do, I made all the beds and dressed my little brothers and myself. Soon our friend, Dr. Hebert was there. It was true, our baby had died, probably of what is called "crib death." Anguish still sweeps over me as I recall the stretcher carrying away that tiny little form, with one

Go! You Are Sent

little foot sticking out of the sheet that covered him. They took my little brother away on a stretcher. It all seemed unreal.

Daddy was getting ready to take a shower. Mom greeted the friends and neighbors who arrived to offer help and consolation. I went up to my father, he looked at me with his eyes red with tears.

"Why did God have to take our baby?"

"I don't know, Daddy, I don't know," I moaned.

We hugged and cried together for a while.

Grieving didn't fit my dad. These tears over the loss of Robin didn't detract from his strength, but it wasn't like him. He always told me to "bite the bullet." Dad navigates to the shores of safety in the troubled waters of life through the channel markers of a quick wit and an enormously generous heart. I loved him and I knew he loved me. All of us thought he was the greatest and we repeatedly overlooked his shortcomings.

I focused on the trip again as our car slowed down.

Before I had a chance to get too lost in my memories, Daddy pulled over and said, "You'd better dry your eyes, I'm stopping for gas. We might as well have lunch."

We had already crossed the Atchafalaya Swamp. Ordinarily, this was the part of the trip to Baton Rouge that I liked best. I loved the way the blue skies and clouds were reflected in the dark, murky waters. Sometimes you could spot an alligator and always there were ripples from fish that jumped at the surface. The swaying of the soft, drooping branches of the cypress trees in the summer breeze made the Atchafalaya basin seem harmless. But, seasoned Cajun fisherman warned newcomers that getting lost in the labyrinth of waterways could be dangerous. Today, as I headed for a new life at LSU, I hardly noticed that we had driven by my favorite scenery.

We stopped for lunch.

A Place of Beginnings

Cajuns love seafood. All that emotion had given me an appetite. I finished off a fried shrimp platter in record time. As we drove off for the second leg of the trip. I picked up the frame again.

Another photo I had put in my collection was of Mama cooking at Kisinoaks. She's the world's best Cajun cook, no doubt about it. Whoever said that good things come in small packages, must have had my Mom in mind. She's a real homemaker, too. It just comes naturally to her. I couldn't wait to see how my room at LSU would turn out after we decorated it together. Mama can walk into a strange room and, suddenly, with a swift switch of furniture, a touch here and there, it's not a strange room anymore.

Looking at the photographs had started me crying again. "Please turn the radio on, maybe if I start singing, I can stop crying." I asked Dad.

Daddy turned on the car radio and glanced over his shoulder. "Is that loud enough?"

"Yes, thanks," I said.

Suddenly, the top of the Capitol Building appeared over the tops of the trees. Louisiana had the tallest state capitol in the USA. That landmark sits at the edge of Cajun country, and always triggered a surge of excitement for me. For the time being, Kisinoaks' tug subsided and I was energized.

"It won't be long now, there's the top of the Capital. Maybe if you put those pictures away, you won't miss the ride through 'Tiger town'."

"Okay, Daddy, you're right. But I want to show Mama this one last picture," I said.

"Mom, don't you love this picture of Bruce with the retainer?"

Go! You Are Sent 8

In the center of my collage, was the retainer photo. My brother Bruce was twelve years old on that Christmas. He wore a retainer for his teeth, and he had lost it twice! Braces were expensive.

When Bruce and Daddy talked about Christmas gifts, Daddy had been firm with him, "Sorry son, no big gifts this year. You'll have to get a new retainer."

Bruce didn't even bother to ask for anything else; he was convinced that the retainer was going to be his Christmas gift.

Childhood with all its wonder came rushing back as I remembered the typical Gremillion Christmas morning. Our gifts would be laid out in the living room behind securely shut cypress doors. All of us kids awakened Mom and Dad.

"Merry Christmas, Merry Christmas everybody!" we shouted in unison as we smothered them with kisses.

"Now can we go to see our presents, please, please?" Rachel would say.

"They have to get their coffee *first*. Don't you remember?" one of the others would explain.

Then came the protracted, but exciting wait as they got their cups of coffee and readied the camera. Daddy would go into the living room first, and as we ran in to see the gifts, he took pictures.

The Christmas of the retainer, there were bicycles for Brian and Jed, dolls for Rachel, clothes for me, and one small game of checkers for Bruce. On top of the checker game was a little envelope.

"That's your gift certificate for one retainer," Daddy said as he noticed Bruce's failure to open it.

Bruce mustered up a smile, turned to Brian and Jed and said, "Those are great bikes. We can go riding this afternoon, okay y'all?"

"Thanks for the new retainer, Daddy, I'm going to hang onto the new one!" His brave attempt at gratitude made him seem pretty grown up for his twelve years. Somehow, we knew he'd make it through braces. "And I really like the checker game." Everyone else in the room swallowed hard.

Finally, Daddy said, "Bruce, look on the back of your gift certificate."

The gift certificate read, "Good for one retainer." On the back of the card it read, "Look outside on the front porch!"

Bruce read that part out loud, and we were all close on his heels as he scurried outside to the front porch, where there awaited him the neatest little black and red go-kart! On the back of the driver's seat was painted the name, "Bruce's Retainer." He made a beautiful flying leap right into Daddy's waiting arms amidst our shouts of joy and laughter.

"That's one Christmas, I'll never forget," I told Mom and Dad. "I wonder what this Christmas will be like when I come home from college. I hope Christmas morning will never change."

I finally put the frame away. We were almost there. I took out my makeup bag and freshened up my lipstick. I snapped my compact closed. I got out the letter that had my room assignment on it. Now, I was truly getting excited. I wondered who my roommate would be. I hoped my classes this summer would be fun.

At my high school, I'd been class president for three years, and graduated salutatorian. At LSU, I planned to set the world on fire academically, and then go on to medical school. I wanted to be involved in medical research. My fantasy was to be a doctor in a research lab. Like the majority of the youth of the sixties, my daydreams involved California. The lab of my imaginings was not just an ordinary laboratory. I wanted to discover the cure for cancer in a redwood lab overlooking Big Sur.

The mental picture of myself in a lab coat, looking into a microscope, and scribbling away about some jealously guarded medical secrets captured my thoughts. The memories that I had pined over just minutes earlier faded into the background. I bounced back to my usual exuberance.

"Coming to summer school is going to be really cool, I just know it. I think I made the right decision," I declared to my parents, who knew all along that I'd perk up as we drove onto the campus of the top party school in the nation.

"And the decision to come this summer had nothing at all to do with a certain LSU athlete, right?" Mom chided.

"Not at all!" I scowled. "Besides, he's not coming to summer school."

This was the opportunity I had been waiting for to ask my parents if my friend could join us for dinner in Baton Rouge that night.

"Now, that you mention it, can he have dinner with us tonight? He's leaving for two months and I want to say good-bye," I asked, trying to sound casual about it.

"Sure, why not?" Daddy answered. He liked him.

Chapter Two

Big Sur Lost

Earth shaking events were about to shape my future —not in the successes of my fantasies, but in the heartbreaking trial of being an unwed mother. My arrival at LSU and the conception of my baby were practically simultaneous. Swept off my feet and succumbing to my own weakness, I found myself pregnant and alone.

The baby's father was only nineteen, and although we had talked about marriage, our relationship was not as solid as it should have been. We had both seen other people between the time of conception and the time I realized that I was with child. We struggled to cope with our dilemma. He said that he wasn't sure that he *was* the baby's father. We couldn't bring ourselves to tell our parents. He brought me to a doctor who saw the girlfriends of the LSU athletes. The doctor and his nurse arranged an appointment for an illegal abortion for me without even consulting me. They assumed that was the purpose of my visit. That offered a quick remedy, a way out. I was confused by my fears and crushing disappointments —in myself, and in my relationship. I insisted on being driven in front of the place on the night before the abortion. I groped for an answer. Terror welled up in me as we drove by. It looked like an ordinary house in an ordinary middle class neighborhood, but I will never forget it.

"No way, there is no way I can go in there. It's just not right," I said to the baby's father.

Without realizing that I had distanced myself from him as we approached this threatening house, I suddenly noticed that I was all but hanging out of the passenger side door. He reached across and put his hand gently on the nape of my neck.

"Look, I love you. I won't *make* you do this. Don't you think we should go on with our lives and finish school? We can get married after I finish. This would be better for you. You won't even have to tell your parents." He sounded convinced.

"I can't do it! I wish I could die! That would solve it. I'm sorry," I said with tears streaming down my face.

We drove back to the dorm in strained silence. Thank God, I couldn't kill my baby. The more we tried to sort things out, the further we grew apart. Finally, we stopped seeing each other. He came back months later, for one more try, but my heart had already been broken.

I didn't tell my parents. For six months, my interior life was a tightrope act. I was hiding an un-hidable secret. If I had only known, then, the ways of God; if only I had valued chastity; if I had only received some Christian counseling, I could have been spared so much anguish.

My academic hopes were dashed by my predicament. The charade of being a typical college coed wasn't too hard to manage during summer school. I was a fairly convincing actress. Morning sickness was the hardest. If I got caught throwing up, I pretended I had too much to drink the night before. It was during the summer break at home that things got tough.

Dad and Mom were very tolerant of my "C" average, and were just happy that I was having fun at school, or so they thought. What I didn't know was that Dad had arranged for me to be in the "Miss Abbeville" contest.

"The TV cameras are out there. Daddy's out there with Rachel and the boys, we've got a big cheering section. Don't be nervous," Mom told me as I approached the runway.

"Okay, Mom," I said smiling. Inside, I had such mixed emotions. I knew my parents would be so proud if I were selected, but the secret of my pregnancy haunted me.

I won the title of "Miss Abbeville," and all the time I was thinking, "Why am I doing this? If they knew about this little baby that is now kicking inside of me, they would be shocked!" The secret got more complicated in the fall semester when I was elected to the beauty court and presented at the Gumbo Ball. I had to have my ball gown enlarged. My secret weighed heavily.

When finally I did tell my parents they were overwhelmed. Their hopes for me were dashed too. Their major disappointment was for me. Because I was six months pregnant, I was able to convince them that the relationship between the baby's father and me was over. Marriage at that point was not an option. Being part of such a connected family, it was agony to imagine giving up my baby. My parents took me to see a priest in New Orleans.

"She can't think only of herself at a time like this. The baby is the one to be considered," he said to them in my presence without looking at me. It was like I wasn't there.

"You live in a very small town. The child would be scarred by his illegitimacy. But don't be discouraged, this can have a very happy solution," the priest continued.

"What kind of happy solution? What do you mean?" I asked.

"There are countless young couples praying for babies to adopt. God knows, this child needs a life where it can find the love, security, and provision of a whole family," he answered kindly. "I've helped lots of girls in your situation. The infant homes are usually run by religious orders and there is total confidentiality."

"He's right, I can't give him a real home. Gossip and shame *would* be heaped on us in Abbeville. Adoption *is* the best thing for the baby," I said to myself, being as persuasive as I could.

We let ourselves be convinced. Besides, thirty-one years ago there were so few "solo moms." A family meant a mother *and* a father.

Daddy had a favorite aunt and uncle in Kansas City. We decided that I would fly up and stay in St. Anthony's Infant Home. Aunt Betty and Uncle Henry would be there like family for me, in my time of need. It was a major relief to be in that home for unwed mothers. The nuns that ran it were strict, but very kind. I was no longer the world's greatest sinner. There were other young women who had come to the same situation, the same heartbreak, the same shame.

Best of all, in my new "home" I was alone with my baby. I could blush with pleasure as he kicked. I could hold my hands over my tummy as he clumsily changed his position. I could daydream about who he would look like. I could talk to him and tell him I loved him.

One night, a few weeks after I arrived at St. Anthony's infant home, I went downstairs to the chapel to pray. The life in the home lent itself to getting in touch with God. There was order, prayer and work. The chapel felt wonderfully warm, the silence and candlelight wrapped around me like a shawl. Jesus was there, I couldn't see Him. But I knew He was there.

"Lord Jesus, the problems of my life are just too much for me. I'm young and I already feel old. I don't blame anyone but myself. Sometimes the pain in my heart takes over completely. I can't feel anything else. Other times, I feel empty. Help me, please! Give my baby good parents. Help me to keep out of trouble." I prayed in total honesty.

"Dear God, I've decided what I want in life. I don't want to be a famous research doctor in a redwood laboratory overlooking Big Sur. I don't want to be a doctor at all anymore. I want to get married to a good man and live happily ever after. Please find me a good husband."

I prayed through the intercession of St. Anthony, the patron saint of lost and found. I wanted to find a good husband. Actually, I didn't want to go looking, I wanted him to find me!

My baby son was born on March 26, 1962, right after midnight. I named him Jude Gerard. I only got to hold him once. I rocked him and gave him a bottle. I smothered him with kisses. I smoothed his hair, counted his toes. I whispered in his ear, between my painful sobs, "I love you. I love you, my little baby."

They wouldn't let me take a picture of him. I held him facing me. I wanted to have the image of his precious little face seared into my memory. I clutched him tightly to my breast and whispered again in his ear, "Don't be afraid. I will never forget you. I'll always pray for you."

The first two months after I surrendered him inched by, minute by minute and hour by hour. An incredible pain of separation found a crevice in my heart and padlocked itself in. I could not grieve in public. I cried into my pillow. In my loss, I found consolation in solitude. My parents prayed for me.

The resilience of youth is amazing. Once I had talked my parents into letting me contact the social worker; once I had an assurance that my baby son had gone home to his new parents, I regained strength and even enthusiasm for life. I dieted back into my pre-baby figure. I walked in the woods and under the stars at Kisinoaks. I taught Rachel to dive in our

Go! You Are Sent 16

pool. I raced up and down the bayou in the speedboat named after me. Friends came around as if nothing had happened. I made plans with my cousin Mickey to attend Nursing school in New Orleans in the fall. There were rumors about me in Abbeville, but time passed and my secret remained in my heart.

God's plans for my life began unfolding shortly after I arrived home in early April. I decided to attend summer school at USL, in Lafayette, the Université des Acadiens.

Cajun country's own university had been the courting grounds of my parents. The magnificent live oaks stood staunch guard over traditions and young love. The lazy cypress lagoon teemed with subtropical fauna and flora. The friendly Cajun folks from professors to policemen were like the hands of God reaching out to me that summer, the summer of sixty-two, in a touch of healing.

Chapter Three

Future Full of Hope

A lifetime had happened since my high school graduation. I was still a typically impulsive, passionate Gremillion, but the surrendering of my baby had sobered me. I grieved and could tell no one. At times I thought the pain would actually kill me. I had a truly adult sorrow to deal with and real help could come from only one source. I reached out to God again. He was still there. I hoped for the best. I was ready to get serious about my future. Summer school at USL began in early June, and the Charity Hospital School of Nursing had gotten in touch with me. I was accepted.

As I shampooed my hair the Saturday morning of the Memorial Day weekend, I was interrupted by the ringing of the telephone.

"Hello," I said. The earpiece got full of suds.

"Hello, may I speak with Genie, please?" a wonderfully deep, male voice asked politely.

"This is she," I answered, not recognizing the voice.

"Genie, this is Frank Summers. Do you have time to talk?"

By this time, I'm wiping my face and neck with the bottom of my shirt. The floor and my back are slippery from my dripping head. Had it been anyone else, I probably would have asked them to call back in a few minutes. But at the mention of his name, my heart pounded at my rib cage.

"Frank Summers, what a surprise! It's been two years since you left Abbeville, right?"

That voice suddenly transported me to a Mardi Gras holiday when I was just a freshman in high school. Everyone has a perfect romantic memory. Mardi Gras of 1958 was mine. Several Abbeville families had rented an entire floor of the Monteleone Hotel in the French Quarter of New Orleans. We watched the opulent parades and avoided the crush of revelers in the posh comfort of our private hotel balcony overlooking Royal Street. Frank and I had come with our families. He won my admiration by the way he handled himself and his restless brothers and sisters. Admiration developed into a secret crush that lasted throughout high school. Our paths intertwined at Mt. Carmel High, and I managed to spend some time alone with him on speech tournaments and French festivals. My rival in those days, however, was totally out of my league. Frank was head over heels in love with the great outdoors.

"I saw you at the Candlelight Lounge last Christmas, but you looked like you had something on your mind. You didn't see me." Frank's words brought me back to our phone conversation.

"Last Christmas? Sorry. I really didn't see you. I *promise* I'd have gone over to talk to you. When did you get into town?" I asked. He lived in New Orleans now with his family.

"Last night, when did you get back?" he asked.

Obviously he didn't know I had not attended LSU in the spring. That was both good and bad. It meant he hadn't heard the rumors, but it also meant I needed to explain staying out a semester in my freshman year.

"I've been back for a while. You see, I wanted to change my major from pre-med to nursing, so I went to spend some time with my Aunt Betty in Kansas City. She's a nurse. I've been back since Easter." I perspired as I lied. It was a fairly plausible explanation and I had only been away from Abbeville for two months. I always worried that people would dig for details.

"What've you been up to since then?" he asked.

"Swimming, working at Dad's office, and driving the boat. Nothing too exciting, just enjoying the family," I answered, relieved that he didn't investigate the missing two months.

My hair was drying into a mat of hardened suds as we talked for about an hour. Something clicked in our conversation. Frank was far from superficial. He was interesting and he was mature for his years. Feelings that I thought I'd be afraid to feel again, slowly entered the fragile spaces of my heart. All past romantic relationships seemed like shooting stars in comparison to the galaxies of emotion and respect I felt for this man whose voice wove a cocoon of security around me.

"How do you like living in New Orleans? Do you miss Abbeville?" I asked.

"I miss Abbeville all the time, especially the house I grew up in near the woods," he answered with a hint of sadness.

"What do miss about it?" I questioned. I wasn't just asking. I wanted to know him a lot better.

"I miss it most in Autumn," Frank explained. "When I was little, I walked the woods for hours. Squirrels jumping from tree to tree, golden red leaves crunching, a chilly wind blowing. For me, that was heaven. Did you know that most songbirds are migrating through Louisiana in the fall? Up north they equate spring with songbirds, but I think of them in the fall."

"My favorite thing about fall in Abbeville is the smell of Steen's syrup cooking in the mill on a chilly day," I said describing the best smell in the world.

"Man, you're right, there isn't anything like that in New Orleans!" he concurred.

"Out here at Kisinoaks, I love the bayou and walking in woods. You remember Sister Bartholomew?" I asked.

"Sister Bartholomew, the junior class English teacher?" he responded.

"Yes, she entered my poem in a national poetry contest when I was a junior. It's called 'Woods After a Rain.' I'll read it to you one day if I can find a copy of it. I guess loving the woods is something we have in common, right?" I asked happily.

"Yeah, I know what you mean. I had my own world in the woods. Except that Pres and my cousin Billy hunted and fished with me. You name it, we conquered it. We'd come back right at dusk, running like crazy with the cold evening air on our faces," Frank said. He made it sound like fun as he told it.

Louisiana in the sixties was known as the "Sportsman's Paradise." Boys and men were expected to hunt, and fish. Even though I was a girl, my Daddy had taken me along on some of his hunting and fishing trips too. Frank and I had that love in common. You can hardly live in Louisiana and not be tuned into the love of nature.

By now my shirt had dried and I was lying down on the carpet with my feet up on the wall. One of our main topics was family. His brother, Pres, was his best friend. My cousin, Mickey, was mine. She was a year younger and we planned to go to nursing school and room together in the fall. I still had a medical career in mind. Frank planned to go to law school. We'd both be living in New Orleans for a while. That sounded good to me!

"How long has your family lived in New Orleans now?" I asked.

"Dad's been on the Supreme Court now for almost three years. We stayed in Abbeville the first year, and I was at

Springhill College the second year. So, I've only lived there this year while I went to Tulane," he said.

Frank's dad first was a lawyer then was elected trial judge, and later a Justice on the Louisiana Supreme Court. Judge Summers was highly respected as a jurist, and a strict interpreter of the law. He was intensely immersed in his work. (He retired as Chief Justice in 1980.)

It wasn't that his dad was a Supreme Court Justice, but something about the way his family valued integrity impressed me deeply as we talked. I felt myself really glowing; it was the glow a woman feels when her man is around.

"Hold on, Genie," I said to myself. "It's just a phone call."

Finally, he got around to the original purpose of his call.

"I'll be going to summer school at USL this summer, and I wondered if you'd like to go to a movie with me next Saturday night?"

Frank Summers was asking me for a date. I was one happy girl.

"Next Saturday? That sounds fine. I'll be looking forward to it," I replied trying not to sound too anxious.

"Great, I'll call you next week to tell you what time. I'm staying with my grandmother this summer. I have to go back to New Orleans tomorrow to pack up. I think my parents are going to buy me a car to commute from Abbeville to USL. Maybe we can ride to school together sometimes?" he suggested.

"I'm commuting with some of my girlfriends, but sure, maybe we can ride together sometimes. Thanks."

The week seemed to last forever. I couldn't wait for Saturday to come. Early Saturday morning, I got up and baked some chocolate chip cookies for the family.

Go! You Are Sent

22

While the cookies were cooling, I looked at myself in the mirror —what was I going to do about my hair?

I had gotten one of the "in" haircuts, called the "artichoke." It was supposed to be easy to keep up and easy for swimming. I loved to swim, but this hairdo was a disaster!

"Maybe rollers would help," I thought to myself.

I jumped in my little purple Renault and went out to buy some brush rollers, wearing an oversized pin-striped oxford-cloth shirt and a pair of blue jeans cut off at the knees. It was rare that I left the house without makeup. I was sure I wouldn't bump into any kids my age. My friends didn't go shopping at nine o'clock in the morning.

I was barefoot. (I was generally barefoot in the summer.) My plan was to slip in and out of the supermarket as fast as I could and rush home to remedy the disastrous artichoke.

Just as I rounded the corner near the checkout counter, who should I bump into but Frank and my cousin, Fofeit! I wanted to hide, but it was too late. They walked up to me.

"I like your shoes," Fofeit said.

"Thanks, they're really comfortable."

I couldn't believe this was actually happening. Frank hadn't called since last week to confirm our date.

"He'll probably change his mind right now and tell me to forget the whole thing," I thought miserably.

He didn't.

He said, "We're here looking for some Ray Charles albums. There aren't any left. I guess we'll go to the record shop. Is it still on for tonight?"

I breathed an inward sigh of relief and answered, "Yes, I'm looking forward to it."

I wasn't going to play hard to get, I wasn't going to "play" anything. Sick of playing the superficial and shoddy games of a party school, I had a longing to be myself.

We talked a little while, and then I said, "Why not bring your new albums over to my house?"

"I've already been seen in my 'artichoke' haircut. He didn't change his mind about tonight. I might as well enjoy the morning, summer school starts Monday," I thought.

They followed me home. We drove up to the kitchen door entrance. The maid and the kids were in the kitchen. The platter of my chocolate chip cookies was cooling near the door.

My little brothers crowded around as the older guys walked in. They wanted to be introduced. The moment Frank walked through the door, I felt like he'd been there a hundred times.

Before anything else could happen, he reached over, and helped himself to one of the cookies. Instead of appearing rude, he did it matter-of-factly, naturally.

I loved it. That one action said volumes to me! It was so unpretentious. I smiled at him, wondering if the glow I felt was visible to him. Frank was at home in my home —and I was falling in love over a chocolate chip cookie!

That night on our first date, the brush rollers had helped. I felt a lot less like an artichoke. Our morning listening to Ray Charles albums had broken the ice and I knew we would have fun. He wore a navy blue poplin suit and I wore a navy and white linen dress. We dressed up for Saturday night dates in Abbeville.

The movie we saw, *Rome Adventure*, was delightfully romantic. Later, my girlfriends compared Frank and me to Troy Donahue and Suzanne Pleshette who were the stars of that movie. We didn't really look like them, but Frank was tall and blonde and I was tiny and brunette. After the movie, we went dancing. Our first date held all the ingredients of an unforget-table evening. I could hardly wait to tell Mama and Daddy about this man that God had sent me.

Breathlessly, I ran through the house. Even though it was past midnight, I opened their bedroom door, flung myself across their bed and announced, "He's the one I'm going to marry."

Daddy smiled and said, "I'll bet you five hundred dollars, you won't marry Frank Summers." (I accepted his bet!)

"What was so special about tonight?" Mama asked.

"Everything. He's just really neat. The movie was about Rome, he loves to travel, and we talked about going to Rome someday."

"Where did you go after the movie?" Daddy asked.

"To a club in New Iberia. He's a good dancer, almost as good as you are, Daddy," I said smiling at him.

"But it was more than where we went and what we did. I think we hit it off really well. He's coming over tomorrow to swim, okay?" I asked as I slipped out of bed and headed upstairs to my room.

As I lay in bed that night, I remembered my prayer in the chapel at St. Anthony's Infant Home. Could God be answering my prayer so soon? I wasn't sure I would win the bet I had made with Dad, but I was sure that I could never in a million years marry anyone more wonderful than Frank Summers.

Our courtship was like an Acadian fairy tale. Within a few weeks I stopped commuting with my girlfriends, and then Frank and I went to school together every day. We spent as many hours together that summer as possible and we were not the slightest bit bored.

Summer flew by. Bayous and coulees, swimming and horse-back riding, willow trees and pastures were the backdrop for our love story. Hours and hours of absorbing conversation and hours more of silent company-keeping helped us to appreciate the gift we were to one another. We enjoyed meals with my family and his. We explored the Cajun countryside, the woods, and our hopes and dreams for the future.

Shortly after I arrived at nursing school in New Orleans, Frank and I were sitting on the sea wall of Lake Ponchartrain. We loved to watch the sailboats. He was a junior at Tulane majoring in English and planning for law school after graduation. I was really happy that it turned out that we were in school in the same city. Each day, the time we spent apart seemed longer. We had talked about spending the rest of our lives together, without officially becoming engaged. That day on the sea wall, I knew I had to tell him.

Frank had to know from the outset of a serious commitment about the baby. I knew I could trust him with my secret, even if we decided not to marry. I could discern the hurt in his eyes. He was pained by my story. Beyond the pain, he offered understanding and sympathy. He was sorry that the girl he loved had undergone that kind of suffering.

"Frank, I haven't even told my brothers, or my grandmothers. Mickey knows, but I haven't told any friends. If this makes a difference for you, if you think it would be harder for you to love me, feel free to end our relationship. I mean it. I would die, probably. But I don't want you to feel like you can't change your mind about us," I said seriously.

"Look, Babe, for awhile now I've sensed that you had something like this to tell me. I wouldn't have guessed about the baby, but I knew there was something," he told me, and put his arm around my shoulder.

"I guess I'm **pretty** readable, huh?" I said.

"Honestly, this will not change my mind, not in the least. I love you and I want to marry you. I want us to grow old together," he said giving me a squeeze.

One night last March when I was at the home, I prayed that God would find me a good husband. You are the answer to that prayer. I love you. I love you so much," I said snuggling close.

"Did I ever tell you about my conversation with Pres before I went to live in Abbeville for the summer last year?" Frank asked.

"No, I don't remember you telling me," I answered.

"He had asked me about my plans for the summer, and I was very clear. I told him, 'Pres, I'm going to go to Abbeville, date Genie Gremillion and marry her.' What do you think of that?" he asked with a wonderful smile that vanquished my earlier fears.

"It makes me wonder if you always get exactly what you want," I said pinching him on his chin.

"Only when it's something I *really* want," he said still smiling.

"Well, I'm very glad you really want to marry me, how about tonight?" I asked teasingly.

"You just want to get out of that pharmacology test!" he said pulling me to a standing position, and giving me a kiss.

We were engaged officially on Mardi Gras day in 1963. Our parents wanted us to hold off our marriage until Frank had graduated from law school. That would have meant a four year wait. We were young. We wanted to be married before Frank entered law school.

The relationship Frank had with the Lord in high school had waned at the university. Nevertheless, we were making a lifetime commitment. We consulted a priest and asked him to marry us secretly. He wouldn't bend the rules. Frank's parents wouldn't relent. They didn't give their consent —so we eloped.

We drove to Bay Minette, Alabama to be married by a probate judge. Alabama allowed girls to be married at eighteen without parental consent. I was nineteen. Frank was twenty.

The directions to the judge's house were given to us by a nursing student from Mobile. They were incorrect and we ended up asking directions from a police officer. We drove up to a lovely white house with a Victorian, gingerbread trimmed porch that wrapped around three sides. The high ceilings and the breeze from the bay gave the room a feel of cool comfort. The lace curtains rippled in the wind. An embroidered doily in the center of a baby grand piano was graced with fresh flowers in a cut crystal vase. We were nervous, but we experienced a peace and a sense of joyful anticipation as the judge's wife directed us to a Duncan Phyfe dining table to sign the papers.

The judge pulled a small pulpit from the side of the room to the middle of the reception area. I was really grateful for the formal touches.

I wore a white pique suit, a small pillbox hat with a tiny hint of a veil and an orchid corsage that Frank had given me. For the traditional "something blue," I wore a frilly bridal garter. My mom's father was accidentally killed when I was almost a year old. Mom had kept his wedding ring for the first grandchild to get married, and I had taken it with me for the occasion. Frank still wears my grandfather's golden wedding ring. That was our traditional "something old."

It was a beautiful service. The judge's wife read a scripture passage on love from the Bible. The judge stood before the pulpit and we stood facing him.

"Before God and the Probate Court of the State of Alabama, do you take this woman to be your wedded wife, to love and to cherish, to have and to hold, in good times and in bad, in sickness and health, for richer or for poorer, from this time forward 'til death do you part?" he asked Frank.

"I do," he answered looking at me with love and commitment.

"Before God and the Probate Court of the State of Alabama, do you take this man to be your wedded husband, to honor and obey, to have and to hold, in good times and in bad, in sickness and in health, for richer or poorer, from this time forward 'til death do you part?" he asked me.

"I do," I said squeezing Frank's hand tightly and fighting back the tears of joy.

"I now pronounce you man and wife. You may kiss the bride!" he proclaimed.

We were married on May 11, 1963.

On our wedding night in Biloxi, Mississippi, I came out of the dressing room in puffs of white silk and lace. Frank took me by both hands and said, "Let's kneel down and thank God for our marriage."

We knelt and Frank prayed, "Thank you, God, for my beautiful, beautiful wife." My eyes moistened with tears of joy.

After we broke the news to our parents, mine began to insist that we seek the blessing of the Church on our marriage. We agreed to it and sought out the pastor in Abbeville. Father Martin steered us through some rough waters but finally arranged our church wedding to take place in Holy Name parish in New Orleans. On July 15, 1963, Frank and I were married before the Blessed Sacrament in the small chapel of the Loyola Jesuits. Daddy and Mama were our witnesses. The sun was streaming in through the stained glass windows. I had on the same white pique suit I wore for the ceremony in Bay Minette.

"We've promised 'till death do us part' twice in two months. You're mine forever," I teased Frank.

My parents had driven us to New Orleans. They treated us to a lobster dinner before we drove back to Abbeville for the rest of the summer.

In the fall, Frank started law school at Tulane in New Orleans. We lived in a servant's cottage behind his parents' elegant three story home on Palmer Avenue. In 1962, the nursing students were not allowed to be married, so I had to give up that career. I got a job with the accounting department of Tulane University the first day I applied. It was great, and within walking distance of our cottage.

Living on a shoestring, all we needed was time to be together. We watched sunsets and sailboats. We flew kites and picnicked on the levee of the mighty Mississippi. We fed the ducks in Audubon Park. He studied. I kept house and worked.

Once we had gotten over the hurdle of entering law school and getting settled in our cottage, we really began wanting to have a baby. Our plans to wait until we got out of law school to start our family went by the wayside, and I became pregnant with our first child. What an exciting pregnancy! This was to be the first grandchild on *both* sides. It was hard for us to focus on other things as the due date approached.

Frank never went to church after the first few weeks of our marriage. I continued to go for a while, but soon gave in to Sunday mornings in bed with the newspapers. We went back to spend the summer in Abbeville in 1964. We wanted our baby to be born in Cajun country. On June 15, our beautiful baby was born.

We named him Frank Wynerth Summers III. With three "Franks" around, I was afraid that sooner or later, he would get tagged with a nickname we didn't like. So even before we left the hospital we picked out his nickname, we called him "Beau."

I don't think I've ever seen Frank so excited and happy, before or since; he came into my room beaming. I was presented with a dozen red roses. I thought the proud father would wear out his elbows watching the baby through the nursery window.

Beau got lots of loving attention. He had two sets of unused grandparents, two unused great grandmothers, one unused great grandfather, and nine unused aunts and uncles. He was totally cherished. I read a book, *Teach Your Baby to Read*, by Dr. Doman. And at eighteen months, we began to play the "reading game." This was a game in which you placed oversized flash cards on the floor and all around the house until the toddler could recognize the words and read them. Beau was soon reading scores of words.

He was our pride and joy! We wanted to give him every advantage in life. What we didn't give him then were some of life's greatest advantages —knowing God, and brothers and sisters!

Still, Beau filled our life with hope. God had sent us our son to help us plan for the future. In our feeble attempts to make those plans, we didn't realize we were working within the framework of God's great plan. As the prophet Jeremiah says, He had "plans for our welfare not for our woe, plans for a future full of hope."

Chapter Four

London

In temperament, Frank and I were opposites. I was gregarious and talkative and Frank was a loner and quiet. Extrovert versus introvert; passionate vs. prudent; energetic vs. relentless —these differences plagued us as the rigors of married life encroached on our earlier romantic notions. Tension, resentment, and distrust began to eat away at our unity.

We had completely divorced ourselves from the church. Prayer was not in the picture at all. There was no anchor for our family and the waves and tempests of life were taking their toll. Nothing seemed to satisfy Frank. Nothing was ever good enough, except maybe his Scotch-on-the-rocks and the blaring of classical music on the stereo. In law school, we entertained and went out a lot. We drank and partied. We fought about drinking, and flirting. We accused each other constantly. We were both extremely jealous. We loved each other fiercely but the alcohol and socializing sliced into our marriage like a lawnmower out of control.

After graduation from law school, Frank had decided he wanted to further his legal education before entering practice. We began at that time to plan for post-graduate study in London. However, he wanted to take advantage of his father's position on the Louisiana Supreme Court and to accept his Dad's offer of a clerkship. Clerkship in the Law is similar to an internship.

After a year, we moved to Abbeville, so that Frank could work in another court system. His second clerkship was for Judge Putnam, a federal district judge in Lafayette. Besides the educational opportunity these jobs afforded, they paid good money. Sacrificing easily, we lived on one third of our income, saving for the year of post-graduate studies in London.

Those two years were hard on our marriage. But the lure of a year or so abroad, kept us together. I went back to the University of Southwestern Louisiana, this time majoring in English Literature. I managed to keep house, care for Beau, go to school, enter the social scene, and still bring home a "4.0" average. I had the "world by the tail," or so I thought.

As the time neared, planning for our trans-Atlantic crossing consumed us.

We invited my fourteen year old brother, Jed, to come along with us for our year in London. He would be a good companion to us and to Beau, now four years old. That year would afford to Jed the opportunity to attend an English boarding school. On weekends and holidays, he'd be with us.

Our parents and friends approved of our plans, even though they would miss us. After all, it was a great chance to travel and experience other cultures. Higher education was worth almost any sacrifice.

I took out a four volume set of library books called *How to Travel With Children in Europe*. We bought a beautiful coffee table book that served also as travel guide. *This England* is a timeless classic. A library book on packing efficiently equipped me with a skill that would be a blessing to me all my life. The four of us (and our 1966 Volvo) planned to cross the Atlantic from New York to London on the *SS France*. We would be leaving in August of 1968. I ordered a map of London from the British consulate. When I got the map, I naively circled an area at the very center of that historic city, where we hoped to find an apartment.

We knew adventure awaited us as we advanced Frank's legal career. We were setting ourselves up to "name our ticket." Beau would experience the cultures of Europe. He would receive a wonderful "hands on" education.

Mama and Daddy had mixed feelings about sending Jed with us, knowing that Frank and I had rejected our religion. The one thing Daddy asked was that we not hinder Jed from attending Mass every Sunday. They said he could come if we would help him keep his promise not to miss Mass. (It was amazing how that young boy was faithful to the Lord and to his promise to Dad. All over Europe, in one strange city after another, he found a Mass to attend on Sundays.)

We weren't interested in religion. Without realizing it, Frank and I worshipped idols, but not idols of stone or precious metals. Our idols were enshrined in our intellects: money, education, and success.

The trip over on the *France* helped us enter quickly into the spirit of our European jaunt. The salty, sea air, the cosmopolitan passengers, the air of Old World culture, and especially the French cuisine, made us feel like seasoned travelers.

"Beau, did you really lose your sword?" Jed asked as the shores of England slowly appeared on the horizon.

"Yep, I had it at the movies last night, and now it's gone. I guess I won't be able to fight the black knight."

In Abbeville, while planning our trip, Beau and I had read King Arthur and the Knights of the Round Table together. And, although he was four and half, he was determined he would free England from the ravages of the black knight. We had bought him a toy sword and played along. Now that he thought the battle was imminent, he had suddenly lost the sword.

"That's okay, Son. England is more modern now, the black knight isn't bothering anyone anymore," Frank reassured him.

We all exchanged knowing smiles.

Frank and I leaned over the rails at Southampton. It didn't seem real. Before coming, there had been so much preparation. I studied Europe's art and culture. We joined the Royal Shakespeare Guild. Frank had concentrated on budgeting our money. In order to vary our experience in the Atlantic crossings, we would sail home on the *HMS Queen Elizabeth II.*

We wanted to live in the area that we had targeted at home. By a minor miracle, when we got to London, we rented a two room flat at 22 Brewer St. Our flat was situated over a radio shop and next door to a strip-tease joint. We lived in Soho, on the fourth floor, up a flight of fifty-two steps!

"Mom, fifty-two steps is a lot of stairs to climb. I'm going to get tired. Why is that funny looking toilet out in the hall? Why do they call it a flat if it's so high in the air? What language are those men speaking in the downstairs apartment?"

"Beau, wait a minute, hold it! Soon we'll have all the answers. Didn't you love that ride on the double decker bus? Living in London is going to be fantastic," I said.

The theater district, Piccadilly Circus, and Green Park were practically at our doorstep. We bought a kerosene heater; we had no heat and no refrigerator. The milk stayed cold on the window sill. The toilet was in a little closet (water closet) out in the hall. We played a game of waiting to see who in the family would use the toilet in the morning. The first user got a chilly seat, by the third person it was warm.

Frank and I slept on a bed in the bedroom-sitting room. Jed slept in the kitchen on a folding cot and Beau slept on a mattress on a countertop, also in the kitchen. The countertop covered the bath tub. We all had to clear out of the kitchen when

London

someone wanted to take a bath. The water for bathing was heated by a natural gas heater, right above the tub. There was a meter, which dispensed the gas. It was run sixpence by sixpence. Without a sixpence, you couldn't have a warm bath.

Each day we put away Jed and Beau's bedding in order to have a functioning kitchen. We hauled our dirty clothes on our backs several blocks to wash each week. We put up with a lot of hardship for the sake of higher education.

The tourist attractions became old hat to us. The pigeons in Trafalgar Square came to know Beau. After a while, we were able to shop in Pounds and Shillings. We knew the National Museum almost by heart. London became home. But there was something more.

Our marriage had never been stronger. Sure, we had a few heavy marital scraps, but we learned about coping in a strange world. Stepping out of the "system" for a while, drew us closer together. Our goals for Europe had been clear. Frank's studies, hard and challenging, had been the number one priority. My role was a supporting one.

Our time in Europe flew by, we had made the best of ou time. I found myself in tears the night before we embarke from Le Havre.

"I can't believe, after fourteen months abroad, we're leavir on a ship that will bring us back home," I said. Frank and I held hands and sipped French wine by candlelight in a little Café.

"Why are you crying?" Frank asked.

"I'm just worried that we won't be able to hang on to the closeness, the experience we've shared," I said, wiping my eyes.

"We'll just have to work at it, Babe," he answered.

Go! You Are Sent 36

"For how long? We don't have any power over our lives when we live in the system. You're going back home to practice law. Our professional life is secure. But what about our marriage?"

"I think the Cabernet is making you too sentimental," he said. "We'll be all right."

Early on the day we left, we did our final packing. The hassle of getting ready caused the sentiments of regret to slip into the background. Once we boarded the beautiful, luxurious *Queen Elizabeth II*, our spirits lifted. When the ropes cast off, and the ship set sail, we toasted it with a bottle of Champagne.

Our stateroom was spacious and swanky. There was a discotheque. This purported to be a fun trip. It really began that way. Jed and Beau had a whole new ship to explore. Frank and I expected to get a week of reading and relaxing.

The fun part of the trip halted abruptly as we sailed into a storm. The wind blew harder and harder and the waves got bigger and bigger. The library shelves were emptied of books. Crystal glasses crashed to the floor by the hundreds in the bars and the discotheque. Chairs, with people still in them, went sliding and tumbling across the lounges.

Everywhere we walked, there was evidence of seasickness. The dining room was practically empty. A few waiters, looking kind of green around the mouth, served the meals with great difficulty. Jed felt somewhat sick, but Frank, Beau and I stayed well.

Frank's Dad had been a Captain in the Navy. Their family had owned a yacht, many of our family friends owned deep sea fishing yachts, and we were often guests aboard. Now, on the *Q.E. II*, the ferocious sea frightened us, but only a little. From the glassed-in deck, it was simply majestic.

However, after the storm raged for thirty-six hours, and we began to lurch wildly, Frank sent me to get Beau out of the nursery and to find Jed. He made us all sit on one of the decks very near the life boat station. The great ship was holding its own, but who hadn't heard of the Titanic? In very few situations have I seen Frank alarmed. He is a very sensible, calm sort of person.

"If he's worried," I thought, "I'd better worry, too."

Sitting out there in the middle of the Atlantic Ocean in the storm, I could see that Jed was praying. He had prayed for quite a few things on our trip. His prayers brought results. I hoped the Lord was still listening, we needed Someone to calm the storm.

As night descended, we took the boys to our room and went to the almost empty disco for a drink. The sea was calmer now. The Captain's voice came on over the speaker system.

"This is your Captain. We can be thankful that we are traveling on one of the finest ships ever made. Our arrival in New York harbor tomorrow will be behind schedule. We have been sailing through a hurricane."

I remember thinking, "Now he tells us! They say there are no atheists in a foxhole. Could there be any atheists in a hurricane in the middle of the Atlantic?"

I, for one, had spent time thinking. The stories of Jesus calming the sea came to mind. Man might be clever, but what could man do against the stormy sea. Only God can calm the sea —only He is more immense and powerful than a stormy sea.

On arrival day, the ship's crew got busy cleaning up and repairing damage. My mood had swung, now the four of us were *excited* to see the Statue of Liberty and the shoreline of the "good ole USA."

Dad posted "Welcome Home" signs along the highway for a mile before we reached Kisinoaks! Across the driveway, he had strung a big welcome banner. We drove in about ten in the morning. Hugging Mom and Dad and all my brothers and sisters was sheer joy. Everyone looked so good to us, and the smell of Mama's home cooking was fantastic. There was a pitcher of fresh Bloody Mary's behind the bar. (It's never too early to celebrate in Cajun Country. The demon of alcohol does the backstroke in the pitcher.)

"You look terrific. I like your make up. Where did you learn how to do it?" Little Rachel asked me in the middle of a hug.

"In modeling school, I'll teach you in a couple of years," I said, swinging her around.

Family and friends listened in rapt attention as we told them about our experiences.

"Y'all look the same, but different." Brian observed. "Beau sounds strange too. When do you think y'all will be normal again?"

We weren't too anxious to be normal again. It was nice to be in the spotlight.

Frank's brother, Pres, had married while we were gone. So had Bruce; Liz was my first sister-in-law, that was neat. Some very sad news greeted us as well. Bruce, and Liz's newborn son, my first nephew, had an inoperable birth defect.

"Please pray for him. Pray for Bruce too!" Mom was begging us on the day we arrived.

"Okay, Mom," I answered dully.

Frank's agnostic views were bouncing around in my head. "If there was a God, how could He allow that tiny baby to suffer? If He existed, He wasn't too interested in human beings," I huffed to myself.

Homecoming was wonderful. The kids had grown, we'd been missed. Hunting season for Frank was just around the corner. Life would resume.

Before we left for England, the same year Frank clerked for Judge Putnam, we had lived in the big, two story, colonial style house on Second Street in Abbeville. That house had been the Summers' home before they moved to New Orleans. After we got back from our time abroad, we moved back into the colonial house on Second Street. Before we could get completely unpacked, friends began arriving. As usual, Frank cracked open the beer, and I stood behind the bar mixing drinks.

"Let's go to The Pub —how about dancing the night away?" Our friends asked. They wanted to celebrate our homecoming.

"Give me a minute to change," I said. I rushed upstairs to don my new black suede mini-jumper, accented by my new suede boots and new false eyelashes.

"I wonder if they'll like it," I thought. "I hope I didn't waste my money on modeling school. I'd like to be the first one with the latest fashion for a change."

Several couples were waiting downstairs when I came down.

Some of the guys greeted me with catcalls. The outfit was a hit!

Frank stopped at our bar before we walked out of the door. "Anyone want a fresh one for the road? I'm having a scotch-on-the-rocks," he said.

During the evening, after dancing with our own spouses, we began to change partners. I felt rather popular that night, at first. I don't know if it was the suede jumper, or that I had several stories to tell about London.

I noticed that Frank was visiting an extra long time with an acquaintance of ours at another table. Her husband wasn't there. She was with friends, and looked especially pretty that night in a modest blue dress.

All of a sudden, my cousin Fofiet leaned across the table and asked, "What's the matter with Frank? Don't you pay attention to him at home?"

Tears started rolling down my cheeks. The next thing I knew, my false eyelashes were falling down. It was symbolic to me of the whole of my life. It was coming "unglued"!

"Flirting troubles already? We've barely arrived." I said to myself. Miserably, I thought, "I hate these false eyelashes, the black suede dress. What's so great about talking about our trip? I wish we were back there."

I felt doomed, too. We had lived in this pattern since our early marriage. Drinking, flirting, then going home and fighting about it. Making up and trying harder for a while, then back to the same old sins and failures. It was a cycle of defeat. The dream of some kind of unified family life slipped completely out of the picture as we began to settle back into the "let the good times roll" way of life that characterizes Cajun country.

The handwriting was on the wall. Even though our financial situation after London was better than it had ever been, our family life was in trouble.

Chapter Five

Too Blind to See

"The law is a jealous mistress," Louise, my best friend, said. Her husband had been practicing for a few years now. We sipped our vodka gimlet's and arranged the bud vases for the Vermilion Parish Bar Association's 1970 Christmas party. We had been swapping complaints about our husband's schedules.

"Well, if the law is a jealous mistress during the *week*, on weekends, the stupid *farm* is a fiercely jealous mistress! I'm not sure if it wouldn't be easier to compete with a flesh and blood mistress. Anyway, I'm sick of planning my life around his hunting," I complained.

Frank's parents had an enormous farm, and adjoining land that was a wondrous wilderness filled with wildlife. Since his boyhood, he had spent every moment of his free time enjoying nature, hunting and fishing. I began to spend my "hunting widow" weekends with some single or divorced girl friends.

Frank couldn't leave our family troubles at home. Emptiness and bitterness crept into his work world, too.

One day, Frank came home from the office. He looked discouraged.

"What's the matter, Frank?" I asked.

"I'm discouraged about things at the office. I'm sick of our arguing, I'm tired," he sighed.

"So what do you suggest?" I asked, sounding offended.

Go! You Are Sent 42

"I've been thinking about applying to Columbia Law School in New York, to work on my doctorate," he shared at the dinner table."

"New York! Yeah, Daddy, this time I want to climb to the top of the Statue of Liberty," Beau interjected.

"Maybe after that, I could teach in a good law school. If I were a law school professor. We could live a quieter, more sane life."

I was all for it. I'm pretty impulsive.

"Let's do it. Let's go!" I agreed.

Where Frank went, I would go. In the midst of the agony of trying to live together, we really loved one another. We loved our son, Beau. He was handsome, very bright, loving and great company, even at seven years old.

We didn't have any training on how to live out a marriage successfully. Frank's parents didn't argue, they were too formal for that. Mine did, I thought arguing was expected. But our arguing was killing us.

The one thing we always seemed to agree on was going away together. When Frank suggested Columbia in New York, I remembered London. Would we have another good family year? It didn't take us long to apply, get accepted, resign from his law practice and move up to New York.

The book *New York on $10 a Day* became our guide. We found a little inexpensive hotel on Third Avenue. It had a kitchenette. (Eating out in New York would have killed our budget immediately.) One morning just before dawn, I was awakened by the sounds of pleading and screaming from the adjacent room. I tried to go back to sleep, but then I realized that, due to some quarrel between a man and his wife, she was on the window ledge, threatening to jump. We were up on the eleventh floor. What could I do?!

It was still dark, and the ledges were deeply recessed. I tried looking out of the window. The man threatened to beat her up if she didn't get back into the room. That terrified me. Then I could hear a child whimpering, sobbing, "Please don't jump, Mama."

I woke Frank, who is a very sound sleeper, and asked him if I should call the police. He told me that I shouldn't.

"The hotel management will notice the commotion and call the police themselves," he advised me.

The minutes seemed like hours, I felt so helpless.

Automatically, my childhood relationship with God, which was thrown into gear especially in emergencies, came back.

I begged Him, "Please don't let her jump! Please God, send the police. Please God, help the little girl." Within minutes the police cars were there and policemen were on the street below and at the door to the next room. She didn't jump!

We had begun to look for an apartment. We targeted an area that was in walking distance of Columbia Law School. Beau was registered at St. Hilda's and St. Hugh's, a private school blocks away from Columbia. We wanted him to be able to walk to school. Rental agents assured us this was impossible for our price range. After several days of intense search, we were beginning to think they were right. Because my prayer for the suicide attempter had been answered, I tried again.

"God, please help us! We need an apartment."

"Babe, I think I've found the perfect one. I can walk to Columbia from there and its a few blocks from Beau's school." Frank was elated by his success.

It was the very next day, in the exact middle of our target area and within our budget. I knew that was a small miracle.

Unfortunately, I relegated God again to the role of a God-for-emergencies, refusing to see His constant provision

Go! You Are Sent   44

and protection. New York was not London. It was almost as
foreign to us, but because it was America, we made more
friends.

Being in the doctorate program was good for Frank. Most
of the students were mature, married men. They were highly
motivated and serious about their studies. The professors were
interesting and very well respected in the legal academic
circles.

Frank's field of study was comparative law and legal
philosophy. Despite being serious and cynical, he *loved the
truth*. His seeking of higher education was a seeking as well
for *truth*, a truth that would satisfy a longing within. Everyone
who knew Frank, knew him as a man of integrity.

Frank was inspired by his dissertation chairman, interna-
tionally famous Wolfgang Friedman. Dr. Friedman was recognized for his concern and work for peace and justice. Shortly
after we left, Professor Friedman was attacked, robbed, and
killed only a few blocks from the university. How ironic. That
was New York —the best and the worst walking side by side
each day.

Safety was a big thing on everybody's minds in our neighborhood. Earlier that year, two old women had been killed on
our block.

We were fortunate to live across the street from a little vest
pocket park maintained by the University. There I met several
other young mothers, and we started up the West 113th St.
Block Association. Soon committees were formed. Vigilante
volunteers walked our street at night with flashlights (and
sometimes, dogs) to help the old and the weak walk home from
Broadway to their apartments.

One meeting of the block association was held in our
building. Several people told stories of close calls they had in

the neighborhood. I'll never forget one particular story. On the first floor of our building, there lived an interesting little old man. He was an artist. From my apartment on the fourth floor, I could see that he painted until the wee hours of the morning.

He said that after one of those early morning painting sessions, he went out for a walk. About two blocks away, he was accosted by a desperate looking youth who carried a switchblade knife.

The youth said, "Hey old man, give me all your money!"

The artist replied, "I don't have any money."

The youth answered, "You're lying, old man. And you'd better give that money to me right now or I'm going to rip your guts apart with this knife."

The old man told him, "You wouldn't kill me in front of all these people, would you?!"

"People, what people? Ain't got no people around here."

"Why, yes there are. Jesus is standing on my right side, the Virgin Mary is on my left side, St. Joseph is behind me and the angels are all around me."

Looking more crazed than ever, the young man screamed at him, "You better get out of here, you old, crazy fool, you're crazy, crazy, you know that."

Then the boy himself ran off in the other direction. Hearing the story, the audience burst into laughter and clapping.

Some people wondered where he had gotten such a clever idea. He looked pretty convinced to me; it wasn't just an idea he had on the spur of the moment. I could see that his faith was real to him.

It was a long ten months in New York. We furnished our apartment at the Salvation Army and were quite content with the results. Compared to the flat in London, the place was ritzy.

Again, we scrimped and saved for the sake of higher education. A part time job as a waitress helped me to bring in a little spending money. We took in all the free entertainment at Lincoln Center and in Central Park. We traded off baby-sitting with the neighbors on the rare occasions that we went out. Family and friends thought what we were doing was really great. It's perfectly acceptable to live in near poverty for the sake of education.

The Lord was teaching us about His people. We found that we had a lot in common with people of other nations and races. One of my friends from the restaurant invited Frank and me to accompany her to the Apollo Theater in the heart of Harlem. We accepted. There were only two other whites in the whole theater. At first, we felt slightly uncomfortable. Later, we were practically rolling in the aisle. We couldn't stop laughing at the Honky jokes told by the talented and perceptive comedian. That evening's entertainment helped us see things from a whole new perspective —a real important lesson.

Our friends were from an international group: there was an Indian medical doctor, who was married to a nice Italian girl; we got to know an Irish couple downstairs; friends from Malta taught us to make Eggplant Parmesana. Our favorite couple was a Jewish fencing champion married to a lovely Russian Orthodox lady. They had adopted a Black child.

There in New York, a Greek neighbor introduced me to the literature on the women's liberation movement. Frank had no intellectual objection to the movement. The fruit of my involvement was another matter —the erosion of an already strained relationship.

Through women's lib, I built up sentiments of resentment against a "male dominated system." *Ms*. magazine came marching in and a lot of our love went marching out. It attacked the Judeo-Christian ethic for its denigration of women's rights. I grabbed hold of militant feminist propaganda. I shrugged off the advantages that I had already experienced in a more traditional role of wife and mother.

About that time, we were looking for a law school that would hire Frank to teach law. Maybe inspired by the old artist's story, I began to pray for our future.

"God, this is a real paradox for me —it's hypocritical to pray. We're living a pagan life."

That day Frank came in late, I was angry. But I was also worried. I told him, "Frank, I prayed today that the Lord would help us to get a job or something would happen to show us what to do."

"Comparative law and legal philosophy professors don't move around very much," Frank explained. "I've applied to some law schools for a position. At the interviews, they talk about the positions that will be available in the future."

A teaching position in his field eluded us. One Methodist school wrote him very frankly, "We cannot in good conscience hire an atheist. We are a Christian school."

We left New York. The end of May 1972 —another chapter closed. Leaving the Big Apple behind, we headed South. We were really going to settle down now —no more degrees to pursue, no more uprooting Beau. We were going to "go for it" in Abbeville.

Another married couple hitched a ride with us (our Hungarian friends). They were studying in New York, but visiting relatives in the strawberry growing part of Louisiana. Somewhere in North Carolina, we began to hear a strange rattling sound in the rear of the car. We were loaded down and couldn't imagine what it could be.

Go! You Are Sent 48

Cruising along at freeway speed, Frank said, "We'll stop in about five miles to buy gas, then we'll check on the noise."

The rattling got really loud just before we rolled into the filling station. Frank and the attendant began to check on where the sound could be coming from. Prying off the hub cap, the attendant gave a gasp.

"It's a miracle y'all made it! Three lug bolts have broken off and a fourth one is holding on by a thread! There is only one good lug on the whole wheel!" He kept shaking his head in disbelief.

We stayed overnight in a motel while the wheel got fixed. I complained about the delay and expense, when my friend Genia said, "I think we're lucky just to be alive. Someone is watching over us."

Someone was watching over us, but we were too blind to see.

Chapter Six

Offers Too Good to Refuse

"Let's order some po-boys. Do you still remember how to get to that place near the waterfront?" Frank's dad asked. "Dad, we missed those po-boys while we were in New York, let's take a ride. We can pick up some cokes and beer at K and B," Frank suggested.

"Great, you and I need to talk about your plans anyway," Justice Summers responded.

Justice Summers maintained a law office in Abbeville. He offered Frank the building and the books. Frank entered private practice. With his Dad being a Justice on the Louisiana Supreme Court, and my Dad a successful business man, the financial prospects looked promising.

Things moved fast once we got back. Frank's law practice got off to a very good start. Within a few months of our arrival, he was appointed Assistant District Attorney in charge of the civil parish, Vermilion. We found the right house, bought a new car, and enrolled Beau in Mt. Carmel Elementary, the same school that both Frank and I attended as children.

New house, new car, new jobs kept us busy and satisfied for a while. Materially, things were falling into place for us. What worried us was that we had re-entered the whirlwind kind of lifestyle that had been so destructive in the past.

"Just ignore me, Frank, get lost in your scotch on the rocks. I'll entertain myself. See you later, alligator." I slammed doors and slapped on some fresh makeup one summer night.

Go! You Are Sent 50

"What do you want from me? Can't we just 'live and let live?' You're liberated, I'm tired. Where are you going?" Frank sighed heavily.

Shortly, the old strain on our marriage was back. New twists that seemed to be dealing it the death blow!

Too much drinking, too much outside pressure choked off the vitality of our love. The demands of his practice, the endless board meetings as the D.A. took Frank away from family. My job as society editor of the local newspaper and later as the director of a self-help housing program intensified the crisis.

I was traveling a lot, and growing independent. Frank spent more time in the great outdoors than ever before. Beau spent a lot of time with his grandparents.

Meanwhile, in Abbeville, other kinds of things were happening. These things were happening in the Kingdom of God. The associate pastor of our church parish wrote an article for a national Catholic magazine. *Wildfire in Southwest Louisiana* told about the powerful movement of the Holy Spirit in Acadiana.

Frank and I didn't have a clue about Spiritual Wildfire. We never went to church. We weren't even cognizant that many of our friends and acquaintances were praying for us.

My friend Louise was my most intimate confidant. She converted to Catholicism while Frank and I lived in London. When I returned from New York, she talked a whole lot about spiritual things. I was tolerant, because I loved her. We had dinner together. She and I spent an hour discussing my marriage crisis.

She said, "You know your marriage is in critical danger." Laughingly, but sensitively, she added, "Your fighting in public is getting notorious. Why don't you get some help? I know a wonderful Christian counselor."

Offers Too Good to Refuse

"You can't call it a family anymore. We're just three separate people living in our house together. Frank and I have our own interests and commitments," I explained.

"Well, what do you see as the biggest problem?" she asked.

"We can't stop hurting one another," I answered. "The pain is unbearable. My premise is that we should get a divorce while we still love each other, so that at least we'll be on speaking terms when it comes to dealing with Beau."

It all seemed very logical to me then. Besides, divorce was getting more common all the time.

Louise was worried; Frank and I had such a deep, although fiery, relationship. It was almost unthinkable that we could ever split up. It was like the little girl with the curl right in the middle of her forehead. When it was good, it was very, very good, but when it was bad it was *horrid!* In hindsight, it's easy to see how the battle raged between the Kingdom of Darkness and the Kingdom of Light for our salvation and that of our marriage.

As society editor, I wrote a column full of stinging criticism of Monsignor Martin. He was pastor of St. Mary Magdalen. A pastoral decision he made upset me. That column elicited an avalanche of response, both negative and positive.

What could Monsignor and the dedicated Christians do? Could they hate me and criticize me in return? No, their faith and their Lord demanded that they "love their enemy" and pray for her, and so they did!

At the Kiwanis Club, Frank was called on to bless the food. His response illustrates where we were spiritually. Frank thanked the farmers for their hard work, thanked the shop keepers for their part in handling the produce, thanked the cooks for preparing the meal —a humanistic "blessing" if there is such a thing.

Go! You Are Sent 52

My Daddy, who was a past president of the Kiwanis Club, said, "Frank was very astute at *not* praying, but he managed to make everyone feel like he *was* praying."

What could his Christian friends in the Kiwanis Club do? Could they, as Christians, criticize him and insult him? No, they followed the instructions of the Lord, they did the only thing they could do, they prayed for him.

Louise attended, on occasion, a small woman's prayer group in Lafayette. A guest speaker from north Louisiana happened to be there once. At the very end of the meeting, they were seated in a circle offering petitions. Without mentioning our names, Louise prayed for her good friends whose marriage was on the rocks. She has a gift with words, and I'm sure the prayer was beautifully phrased. She says it was a simple prayer.

Suddenly, the guest speaker said aloud, "I feel that the Lord would have us all stand up and hold hands and pray for a miracle in the life of this couple!"

All the ladies *did* stand and pray for that miracle. Three weeks later, a miracle was granted. Yet, in those three weeks, things got a lot worse in our relationship. Crisis followed on crisis.

I was writing the narration for a film script that I directed for Southern Mutual Help Association. It was a short documentary on a dental clinic in Franklin, Louisiana.

I begged Frank to come with me to New Orleans to review the script and the film. He refused. I felt hurt and rejected.

"He doesn't really like me; I don't blame him; but it still hurts," I told myself. "He never wants to go anywhere with me."

Beau and I stayed at Frank's parents' home. I went out to eat with the film crew and tried to convince myself that this was the life. If I were divorced, I could do *what* I wanted to

Offers Too Good to Refuse

do, *when* I wanted to do it, and be free of hurt and rejection. Frank was at home feeling hurt and rejected, hating me for wanting to go without him. It was a vicious trap.

To expedite the filming of our dental documentary, a driver in a large van took the film crew around the sugarcane plantations. The goal of the trip was to uncover the poverty and oppressed state of the black sugarcane workers who were classified as migrant or seasonal workers on large estates.

We searched for settings that, on film, would best convince the public of the need to support a free dental clinic for the poor.

The cameraman, his friend, the sound man, and I set out on this excursion. The driver pulled up in front of a rather rustic little church. He announced to us, "I would like for y'all to see this little church."

"I never thought of including a church on this film. Hmm. Maybe it would give it a neat touch, a launching place," I said nodding approval.

"Good idea," the cameraman agreed.

"We can't get through the front door. It's locked," the soundman shouted after running up to the door.

We wanted to forget it, but our driver was insistent. We climbed in through the window.

Once inside, stillness and quiet enveloped us. The pews were homemade. Several straight backed wooden chairs, where the elders sat, lined the small sanctuary. On the rough looking pulpit, was the most falling-apart Bible I've ever seen.

We were a talkative group, but here in this humble church, we walked and sat in hushed silence. It reminded me of being at the rim of the Grand Canyon. The grandeur of the Canyon silenced visitors. In this simple place there was grandeur. What was it? What exactly was happening here?

Go! You Are Sent

The driver seemed to have a smiling, secret knowledge. We climbed out of the windows again. We began talking excitedly. *This* was the place to begin the film!

It would show the sugarcane workers at their best.

We turned to the driver.

In answer to our questions, he said, "Yes, I'm sure they will let you film their service. This week is not a regular service. It is a 'Testifying Service'."

I assured him that a "Testifying Service" would be fine, and we'd come back Sunday, ready to film. Sunday came and we were there, bright and early.

The name of the church was the "Bayou Sale Morningstar Baptist Church." Immaculately clean, happy sugarcane workers greeted one another as though they were all one big family. The bell rang and they quickly took their places in the church. They opened with some wonderful gospel hymns. Next, the minister, and one or two of the elders, shared and preached on the Word of God. Then pew by pew, the congregation came forward and stood in front of the sanctuary. They said, "I testify that my family and I are walking in the Way of the Lord Jesus."

Sometimes they would tell a little story of how Jesus helped them to "keep on" walking in the Way. At first, I sat in the back row, observing. Soon, I was listening intently to every word. Later, a visiting preacher began to talk, about the faith of Abraham and Sarah. The preaching was really animated and very stirring. I identified with Sarah's lack of faith. She had laughed when God told her that at ninety years old, she would conceive and bear a child.

I was amazed as the story concluded with the birth of Isaac, the promised son of Abraham and Sarah. I almost applauded. There were many "Amens" afterward, and finally, one elder rose and began to pray petitions. These people were poor and needed help, but the preacher prayed for those who were even *poorer.*

"For the lonely, the shut-ins, the prisoners, those in hospitals and especially those in spiritual darkness." Then he added, "And Lord, please don't forget these white people here. Help them, Lord, save them. Heal whatever needs healing in them, Lord. Take care of them on their way home."

His prayer for us touched me deeply. We had intruded and they reached out to us. The service closed with the hymn, "When I Walk the Last Mile of the Way."

I seldom thought about "the last mile of the way."

Our sound man moved reverently around the church, clearing out his equipment. He held a masters degree in music, he seemed puzzled. "How could poor sugarcane workers, with no special training, harmonize so beautifully?" he kept asking, completely mystified. (We weren't giving the Holy Spirit the recognition He deserved.)

The grandeur of the first visit settled on us again on that Sunday morning. As we regrouped outside the church, the cameraman asked me, "Well, how did you like *that* church service?"

"I loved it! If church were really like that, I'd go all the time!" I said smiling.

That same weekend, Frank received a home visit from a parish volunteer. She was conducting a census about church attendance. Frank was brutally honest about his lack of participation in the Church, but willingly filled out the form. At the very end of the sheet, there was the final question, "In what way would you like to help the Church?"

Frank's carefully wrote his answer —a bitter, tongue-in-cheek comment, "I would like to help the Church in its outreach to the poor and needy."

Go! You Are Sent 56

He knew full well that there was no such outreach, but couldn't resist the sarcasm. Criticizing the Church for its lack of outreach to the poor made him feel justified in his lack of involvement.

The census taker said, "Frank, thank you very much."

That dedicated lady was a real disciple, she knew what God could do, she walked out of our house undaunted, praying and interceding, "Lord Jesus, let it be. Someday let Frank truly have a chance to serve the Church in an outreach to the poor!"

Ingeniously, the Lord had orchestrated a rendezvous between Frank and Genie Summers and *His* servants.

Inexplicably, both Frank and I had declared, out loud in the presence of others, a desire to be more involved in the Church. We were totally unaware, totally ignorant of the power of our own words.

God drew near to a dissolving marriage, His awareness never wanes. He definitely heard us. He knew how desperately we needed to be saved. I can picture Him watching, amused from above, smiling and saying, "These offers are too good to refuse!"

Chapter Seven

Keep Holy the Lord's Day

"People don't really hate corrupt government," Frank was telling me as we drove out to the Summers' family farm. "Some hate it when others benefit from corruption, but just about everyone would like to be able to bend the law for themselves or their families, even accepting public work on private land. You'd be surprised how often I'm asked to 'fix' people's speeding tickets!"

Vermilion Parish was in a dilemma. Several members of the parish governing body were being indicted by the Federal Grand Jury for misuse of public funds. Frank, as the Vermilion District Attorney, had been extra busy lately. He had to be on hand in endless committee meetings.

This day on the farm was supposed to be a real rest for the three of us. But we couldn't help being reminded of the trouble going on in the parish government as we drove past farms whose private roads had been in question.

Frank loved the work in the District Attorney's office. He loved serving the public. God's hand led us over the seas in a quest for the truth. In Europe, his experience began to override his existential philosophy. There, Frank had come to respect his fellow law students who represented many developing nations. Some hailed from India, Pakistan, and Africa. Later, in private practice, he defended indigent clients. Before he knew it, he was developing a real heart for the poor. Active involvement in the Jaycee civic outreaches and the "Rabbit Hill

Renovation Project" awakened in Frank a deeper level of commitment to serve those less fortunate.

He was frustrated sometimes at inequities in the criminal justice system, seeing that those with political pull seldom paid the full price, while the poor and the indigent did.

Apart from corruption in government, the D.A.'s office was cracking down on the rampant drug dealing.

"It's hard to help defendants get a fair shake in the trials, without compromising the state's need to correct and punish criminal activity. That's one of the most difficult parts of the job." He couldn't seem to get his work off of his mind.

The strain showed on his face. I looked over at him and smiled weakly.

Our new Vega sped over the Perry Bridge and headed south out into the country for our day of rest. I could feel the lifting of my spirits. We courted and spent the happiest times of early marriage on the farm.

Louisiana in the summertime is incredibly hot. But the ancient oak trees draped in Spanish moss afforded a wonderful refuge. The usual breeze was blowing. The smell of the summer foliage and flowers, the brilliant, bright blue skies, the sight of cattle grazing contentedly began to tranquilize the tremendous tension that knotted up my insides.

They loved the farm —Frank, Beau, and our beagle hound, "Belle". I resented the place the farm stole from me in Frank's life. But I loved it in spite of myself.

"Look at Belle, Dad. She knows we're going to the farm. She's so excited she can't sit still."

Glancing into the back seat, we saw Belle, squirming and wagging her tail. Beau looked happy. He was only nine years old, but I'm sure he lived in fear of the time bomb that was about to go off in our lives —separation and divorce. Seeing

Keep Holy the Lord's Day

his smiling, hopeful face, shoved a stab of fear directly into my heart! How would he handle this?

Beau had so much potential, and he was a good boy, very much like his dad —serious, strong and honest. Of course, he'd stay with me. He was an only child. Frank was incredibly busy.

I looked over at Frank. I felt so guilty. So much of the problem was me. In trying to come up with some kind of identity, I'd lost my way. I wasn't happy.

Mom told me just days before, "I don't know what's wrong with you! You have become so hard." I couldn't figure out how things had gotten so bad.

There were so many things Frank and I couldn't talk about. A lot of cold silence separated us. The lack of the warm intimate life that had been so sustaining in our courtship, our early marriage, and in London had vanished. There was something eating at Frank. After a few drinks, we'd end up in a shouting match. Poor little Beau, he heard every bit of it. I'd promised myself that I would never do this to my children, and here we were doing it! And what was worse, we couldn't stop. All of our resolutions and thought up solutions had quickly run their course.

We sat on the banks of the canal. The fish weren't biting, so we had our picnic lunch. For the first time in a long time, Frank lay his head on my lap. Beau and Belle went for a long walk. We sat there in silence. The "killer" in this whole situation was that it was impossible to foresee how life would be once we were apart. Hope struggled to the surface, but in agony, I ignored it.

"Why be built up for another let down? Better to get it over with as soon as possible. Let us both get on to a new, more peaceful life. Beau would be better off without having to face constant turmoil." I let my thoughts run. "I'll probably move away. Maybe I can get a good job in Houston."

I lit another cigarette. Frank smoked one of mine. I was irritated that he hadn't brought his own. He picked up his head and propped it up on his arm.

"My cousin Mickey lives in Houston. She's divorced and raising two children. I'll spend next weekend with her. Maybe, I can get a better understanding of what to expect for Beau."

Hours passed. Our sparse conversation was superficial.

"Let's go," I said, "I'm out of cigarettes." On a steady diet of cokes and cigarettes, I was full of nervous energy. I lived with a constant pain in my stomach.

"Probably an ulcer —it'll go away as soon as I get out of this tension and on my own," I said to myself.

I was smoking almost three packs of cigarettes a day. Frank was smoking two packs. I even smoked in the bathtub. I woke up in the middle of the night and lit up a cigarette. I knew that was crazy! These were "The Great American Smokeout" years. Beau, a born activist, wet, punctured and marked our cigarettes. He griped and complained about our habit in an effort to squelch our smoking, but to no avail.

We packed the car and blew the horn for Beau. Soon he emerged from the woods, sweaty and smiling.

"Dad, Belle chased three rabbits, and I got so close to one of them I could've gotten it with my pellet gun. I saw some fox tracks, too, and the tree I sat under had a huge snake coiled up in the branch right above my head. Boy, did I take off running when I looked up." We laughed, got into the car and drove away.

"This is the last time I'll see the farm for a long time —or maybe ever," I thought as I got out to shut the gate.

I blew it a farewell kiss. I didn't want to drive back home to Abbeville. Inside I was crying out, "Stop the world, I want to get off."

Being on the verge of the family breakup was like being at the death bed of a loved one who has been suffering for a long time. I didn't want it to happen, but I didn't want the suffering to go on. Tears welled up in my eyes.

"What's the matter, Mom?" Beau asked.

"Nothing, Baby, Mama's a little sad, that's all."

"You're always sad, lately. Didn't we have a great day?"

"Yes, we did have a great day, Son," Frank answered. "A really great day, I needed to get out like this."

"Frank is just being an ostrich as usual. He buries his head in the sand, and refuses to see what is really going on. How can he be so blind?" Silently, I resented him.

On Tuesday of the following week, I announced that I was going to Houston to spend the weekend with Mickey. Frank hated Houston, or better, he hated my visits to Houston. I had been there several times with divorced girl friends. This time, I was not going with them. I would take Beau, and he would get a chance to see Astroworld. Why discuss it? I was going and that was that!

"Why don't you come?" I asked Frank offhandedly.

I knew full well he would flatly refuse, turn into a block of ice, and walk away.

He did.

The clock on the time bomb was set and ticking. We both knew it. Frank came home for lunch on Friday to see us off. We packed the car in strained silence. Beau was excited to go. Mickey was his Godmother, and he hardly ever got to see her. Donnie, his cousin, was only nine months older, and he was looking forward to being with him. He could hardly wait to see them and visit Astroworld. He was unaware of the purpose of my trip.

"Call me, let me know that you've arrived safely," Frank demanded as we were driving off.

I thought, "He probably thinks I'll wreck the car."

Mickey had just moved to a new apartment and didn't have her phone installed yet.

"I'll call if I can," I said.

We arrived in Houston in the middle of Friday afternoon five o'clock traffic. It wasn't long before reality began to set in. My pumped up pride and my "liberating" independence were being tested. As the city sprawled and tangled before me, I knew that making it on my own was not going to be without its hassles. I finally arrived at Mickey's apartment, pretty deflated.

Mickey and I hugged the kind of hug that contains a whole conversation about heartbreak. I lit a cigarette. She gave me a beer.

Later, Mickey and I left the kids with her sister while we went out to a neat little restaurant in the Galleria Mall to eat and talk.

I needed to unload, to tell her what was going on in my life. Much to my consternation, on the subject of divorce, she didn't say, "Come on in, the water's fine!"

For her, the novelty had already worn off, and the hard, cold facts were beginning to emerge.

"The kids miss their daddy, and to tell the truth, I do too, sometimes. It's hard to be the one always worrying about money. I thought I'd want to date, but that can be a drag, too. I don't think I could make it if I didn't go on trail rides on the weekends."

We ordered another drink.

She asked sincerely, "Why don't you think some more about giving it another try. You say that you still love one another. It can't be that bad."

"Oh, but it is that bad," I said. "It's hell. Anyway, if I don't leave him, I have a feeling that it won't be long before he leaves me. It's inevitable," I countered with a heavy sigh.

I didn't call Frank. It was too much trouble. Besides, I didn't think he'd really care. He was growing more uncaring all the time. He didn't need me. He didn't need friends. He didn't need God —in fact, he disdained the people who used religion for a crutch.

He hunted *alone*. He fished *alone*. He turned the stereo up to a high volume and sat there *alone* with his scotch-on-the-rocks.

Not long before, he'd been to Washington, D.C. on a business trip. He hadn't called me from Washington. Why should I call him now? It was all over anyway.

I was wrong in many ways, but when we married, I had given my heart to Frank. It was broken. He had frozen me out of his life for years now. As a young bride, I remember looking at a National Geographic Magazine with Frank. It was about harems.

Half jokingly I asked, "Would you like to have a harem?"

Always the pragmatist, he answered, "Harems are illegal in the United States, and anyway, they are very expensive."

Not exactly the "I only have eyes for you" kind of answer I expected.

Another time, I called him to meet me for lunch. His mother had taken Beau for the day.

Over the telephone came the serious reply, "Not today. Don't depend on me for your happiness. Make other friends for yourself. Find other interests."

So I took up painting at the Y.W.C.A. Over the years, I kept looking for other interests. Nothing seemed to fill the void. I fantasized about having a week together, just the two of us.

Now I would be doing everything without him. I knew I'd miss him terribly. I couldn't live with him, and I couldn't live without him.

Back home in Abbeville, Frank waited for my call. When it never came, he tried unsuccessfully to reach me. It began to dawn on him that our marriage was really over. For some reason, he thought that I wasn't even coming back from this trip. Finally, he called me. By then, I was furious about being chased down, and the hassle of trying to find a telephone. But, he was accustomed to it. I lived furious.

He questioned, "Are you coming back?"

"Of course I'm coming back, all my clothes are still there. I'll be there with bells on," I told him.

I was shocked as he concluded by saying, "I love you."

"You know something, Frank, I really don't believe you," and I slammed the phone down.

I was crying. I didn't want Beau to see me crying and spoil his fun. But I couldn't keep the tears from streaming down my face as I began the four hour drive home from Houston.

We stopped and bought some Kentucky Fried Chicken.

I thought, "I'd better prepare Beau for the crunch." I began, "Beau, didn't you have fun at Donnie and David's?"

"Yeah, Mom, it was terrific. When can we come back? It takes more than one day to see all of Astroworld."

"You know that Uncle Donnie doesn't live with them anymore. They get to visit him sometimes on the weekends..."

I was building up to the point.

Keep Holy the Lord's Day

"Stop, Mama, I *know* what you're getting at, and I don't want to hear about it! Let's don't talk about that. I want Daddy to live with me."

Another bitter pain gripped my chest. I switched on the radio for distraction. Every channel had a Christian preacher, I was not in the mood for preaching. I lit a cigarette and turned it off. Beau fell asleep as it got dark and I drove on, dreading the confrontation that would surely await me at home.

It was late as I drove into the driveway. The lights were on in the living room. My heart was pounding in dread. I felt badly for slamming the phone down on Frank. I was so tired and deflated. Beau and I entered the house and found Frank asleep on the sofa. Usually, I would awaken him and convince him to go to bed where he would be more comfortable.

But tonight, I thought, "I'll leave him on the sofa. That way we can put off the fight until tomorrow." I whispered to Beau, "Let's not wake up Daddy, okay? You can see him in the morning."

He drowsily agreed and went to his room. I tiptoed around. Just as I was about to slide into bed and turn off the light, I heard a noise and turned around.

Frank had walked into the room.

I looked at him.

He smiled.

All the dread melted away. I was totally disarmed! The argument I had practiced mentally on the way home in the car evaporated into thin air. Frank looked so different. He was a changed man. This was absolutely *not* the man I left on Friday.

"I have something I'd like to read to you. Why don't you come and sit over here by me?"

Go! You Are Sent 66

His voice was so loving and tender, I couldn't resist. We sat there together against the pillows propped up in bed. He read a *seven page* letter he had written to me.

The letter began by asking for my forgiveness for the many ways in which he had failed as a husband and father. It was thorough!

He took upon his shoulders the responsibility for the sad state of affairs we had arrived at in our marriage. As head of the house, he was responsible. Tension melted away as he read. Next, he forgave me for all my sins against him —really forgave me. That was heavy!

My gut reaction was, "Of course I can forgive him. I love him. But him forgive me, that's unbelievable. I don't feel forgivable, I haven't really wanted our marriage lately, I've only wanted out."

He read on, "I love you. We can try again. This time we'll make it."

So many beautiful things were written on those seven pages —healing things, hopeful things.

I was utterly transfixed. There was an aura of unfamiliar peace around us. He ended the letter by saying, "The Lord Jesus will help us rebuild our marriage. We'll try to keep the Lord's day, well —holy. Let's start by going to church on Sunday. God will help us."

"*God* will help us?" I gasped. My mind could hardly grasp what he was saying. This last part was the greatest surprise of all. Frank, who had denied God for so long, was saying that the Lord would help us. What had happened? We sat in silence for a thirty second eon.

"I do love you, Frank. I forgive you. But I don't know if it can work out. What made you say that the Lord will help us?"

Keep Holy the Lord's Day

Patience and passion permeated his explanation. I listened openly. Something *had* happened to him. That was clear.

What I didn't know was that instead of an end of the marriage confrontation, a confrontation of an entirely different kind had already taken place in our sunken living room on Fifth Street. Nothing could have prepared me to hear the story that Frank told me that night.

"I was alone, but not enjoying my solitude," he shifted to face me and yet looked beyond me. "The realization of our marriage breakup shook me up. At first I thought, 'Good riddance, I'll be free to live my life in peace. I'll meet a prettier woman. I'll ...' I was in pain.

"I didn't want to lose Beau," Frank continued.

"Divorce wasn't in the blueprint I'd laid out for my life. What in the world happened? I had planned for us to grow old together. I didn't want *another* family. I wanted *my* family!

"I'd seen poor people oppressed by the system. But tonight, in my misery, I felt like a rich person oppressed by the system. I'd tried my best. I followed all the rules and guidelines —the formulas for success: get a good education, work hard, marry someone that you fall in love with, start a family, travel, seek justice and truth, win a place in the world and live happily ever after.

"Tonight, I was so ticked off, I asked myself, 'Where is the *happily ever after*? What good is all the money I make? I'm successful for a young attorney in Abbeville. So what? Where is the power of money and success to solve this disastrous problem?'

"The futility of it all was crushing me! Despair swallowed me. I was seated on the sofa, and I began to cry. Genie, you've never seen me weep like that. I was really weeping for the first time in my adult life. I thought of suicide. I almost got up to

Go! You Are Sent 68

get my new pistol. I couldn't do that. I couldn't bear to think of the shame that it would cause Beau.

"In my crying, I suddenly had a strong sense that I was no longer alone. Someone else was there with me. I sat up straight and began to dry my eyes. I was so ashamed that someone might see me crying. I looked around. I was alone. No one else was there. I glanced at the door. I thought to myself, 'Who would come over at this hour of the night?'

"I stretched out on the sofa, but as soon as I lay there I started really weeping. I didn't think pain could be that deep. Suddenly, that presence was there again. This time it was much more powerful, much nearer. It seemed to be hovering over me. I felt that I could reach up and touch it.

"It was God. I knew it was God! My despair washed away as the presence of Almighty God surrounded me. Not only did it surround me. It actually flowed into me. God had come to me in my loneliest hour. 'Why?' I asked myself. Instinctively, I knew that the presence of God was not there to punish me. Instead, I felt an incredible flood of love. God was here to love me.

"Again, I wondered why. I hadn't been praying, or looking for God. Still, He was letting me experience His love. I thought, 'Frank Summers, you have nothing at all to commend yourself to God.' I understood inwardly that it didn't matter. God was here, infusing me with peace.

"The realization of my unworthiness swept over me. Frank, the atheist, was being visited by God. The sin of denying God loomed largest of all in my heart. 'Forgive me, God,' I said silently.

"I remembered the nuns, the Mt. Carmel sisters. They had taught me that God came as a person. That *person* was present now. That person was Jesus. I was with Jesus.

"I shouted, 'Jesus, save me. If you are a *saving* God, please save me.'

"Immediately, I knew He heard. He wanted to save me. He was saving me. I could feel it.

"I sat up. I had a million questions. 'What should I do now?' I still felt God's presence strongly.

"Finally, I said, 'Lord, if you save me and my marriage, I'll do anything you show me to do.'"

"Keep Holy The Lord's Day."

Frank's voice dropped a bit, and he said "That's what the Lord said, not in an audible voice, but in a clear, inner voice.

"I was so saddened by the thought of the ten years worth of Sundays that had gone by without my even noticing the Lord's Day. 'Keep Holy The Lord's Day.' I knew that meant I would have to go to Mass —Mass and Communion. In order to go to Mass and Communion, I'd have to go to confession."

I had been listening intently as Frank shared this. There was a sacredness to this moment. Still, the thought of Frank going to confession was hard to capture. "Confession?" I asked. "You wanted to go to confession?"

"Yes," he continued, "I went to the kitchen and switched on the light and found the telephone directory. I doubted that a priest would be awake, but I looked up the number and dialed it.

"There was an answer on the second ring. 'Saint Mary Magdalen, Father Martin speaking.' he said."

"I doubted that he would let me come over, but I asked him anyway, 'Father Martin, this is Frank Summers. I wonder if I could come over right now and go to confession?'"

"Sure, Frank, come over." Father said, " I'll be waiting."

Monsignor Ignatius S. Martin had been Pastor for fourteen years. He'd baptized Beau. Recently, I had criticized him publicly in the newspaper. Now he was involved in the Charismatic Renewal movement in the Parish. Their prayer group was praying for us! Father Martin met Frank at the front door with a warm welcome. They went into his office.

"I told him, 'Father, I haven't been to confession in ten years. I haven't kept a list of all my sins. My soul feels as black as night.'

"Father wasn't shocked even when I said, 'The heaviest weight I feel is the sin of denying the existence of God. I have been so arrogant!'

'God forgives even the arrogant. The important thing is that you're here now,' Father told me.

"I told him that I thought it was too late for my marriage —that you and I are probably going to get a divorce. We've put our relationship at the bottom of the list.

"Father then asked me, 'What makes you sure the marriage is hopeless?'

"I answered, 'We fight constantly. I guess in a way it's my fault. I've left her alone so much and she takes all these damned trips to Houston.'"

Frank looked me in the eye as he said that. I knew he hated my trips. I didn't defend myself. I just smiled.

"Confession has taken on a new format since we left the church. Father Martin and I sat face to face in his office and dug up my sins and failures. He really helped me to understand that so much of my problem stemmed from years of rejecting God's grace," Frank explained.

"You just sat and talked face to face in your confession?" I asked.

Keep Holy the Lord's Day

"Yes, when Father talked to me, he emphasized the healing power of Jesus. He told me 'That was Jesus in your living room, Frank. Jesus doesn't wait until we are worthy to save us.'

'If He did, I wouldn't be here!' I told him, then I asked, 'What now? What can I do about our marriage?'

"Genie, get this, Monsignor Martin told me something that I will never forget."

"What did he say?" I asked.

"He said, 'Frank, if you put *Jesus* at the center of your life, He *will* save your marriage!'

"I left the rectory after confession feeling like a man who hadn't taken a bath in ten years would feel after a long, hot shower —clean to the core. Father Martin's promise that Jesus would save our marriage became more real to me as I drove home. I could sense that the Lord Himself was still present. I prayed, 'Lord, I believe the promise, I trust you with my marriage. But is there anything *I* can do?'

"In that same inaudible voice as before, the Lord told me to sit down and write a letter to you. That's why I wrote that letter I just read," Frank smiled as he patted my hand reassuringly.

Even the hand patting would have seemed absurd four days before, when the tensions in our marriage had been so extreme. I just sat there, overwhelmed with the enormous import of the story that had been told to me.

We broke the silence and then slowly began to talk about our life and the impasse we had come to in our relationship. The entire night slipped by, and we were still talking. Both of us agreed to stay home from work to continue our dialogue. Work had always been first. His willingness to remain with me, his making our relationship a priority confirmed in my heart the change that had taken place. It was a sign.

Go! You Are Sent

Frank drove Beau to school, after he returned he joined me for breakfast in bed. We held hands.

"I really want to *hope* that we can make a go of it," I said dejectedly. "But we've tried everything. I can't believe religion will help."

Frank pleaded, "Then please let me have Beau. You can have your new life in Houston."

Hanging my head, I sniffled and said, "I can't let you have Beau. I'm sorry."

I was sorry, so sorry. The thought of him all alone hurt. I started crying again.

Putting his arms around me, he whispered gently, "Don't worry, even if you and Beau leave me, I will still have *the Lord*."

The truth, the absolute certainty with which he said, "The Lord will be with me," broke the bondage of doubt within me. I cried harder.

Suddenly, eternally, *I heard it*. The voice within. The voice of Jesus, loud and clear.

Jesus said to me, "Genie, this is not the end of your marriage. This is the beginning!"

Freedom burst forth like a geyser. I turned to Frank, our eyes met, we kissed. We laughed for joy. Like a pair of reunited lovers, we embraced.

"Let's really start over. I'll go to confession, too," I said, as new hopeful plans came to mind. "We can renew our marriage vows, and go on a second honeymoon. I'll quit my job, stay home and keep house. We can spend more time together on the farm."

A peace came upon us. The storm had passed. All was calm. We could feel the wonderful presence of God, delivering us from the monstrous evil that had had a stranglehold on our lives.

Frank quickly agreed to the proposals of the renewal of our marriage vows and the second honeymoon. And to my astonishment, said, "Let me make all the arrangements."

My spirit responded. This new determination of his to be responsible for me felt so right. I didn't care where we went, just so we went together.

On Wednesday, I went to confession. For more than an hour, Father Martin and I talked. Father actually evangelized me. I didn't grasp every single thing he said, but I could see he was excited about Jesus.

"Can we come this afternoon to renew our marriage vows?" I queried. His eyes lit up, and he consented gladly.

Frank arrived at the church with a single red rose. Beau witnessed our beautiful ceremony in the rectory. The love of God was tangible. Afterwards, we went into church and knelt at the altar of the Blessed Virgin Mary. I placed the rose on the altar, at her feet. It was August 15, 1973 —the Feast of the Assumption —a Holy Day.

Chapter Eight

We Find a Treasure

"I do remember seeing that Bible somewhere, Frank, but I just can't find it." I called out from the ladder. The top of the closet had a stash of old books that overflowed our library.

"Was it a black one? I remember seeing it too," Beau queried.

"I haven't read it since Scripture class at Springhill. But it seems like I moved it around every time we moved our books," Frank called back.

"I have to go to Mother's to borrow a suitcase anyway, I'll just borrow theirs. They hardly ever use it," I shrugged.

I grabbed my purse and whisked out of the door. Mom and Dad were in Arkansas, but I could get into the house.

Just an hour earlier we renewed our wedding vows. The whole world looked new as I drove out to Kisinoaks.

Soon we would be leaving on our second honeymoon. Frank arranged the whole thing. The Summers were delighted to have Beau for a few days. The Bahamas Islands awaited us. I was tingling with excitement. Frank could manage four days off from work; I cleared five.

Mom's house was quiet, everyone was gone, but I didn't feel like an interloper. I walked past the bar in the den, into the foyer. There at the foot of the stairs, was the big family Bible, laid open to Jesus' teaching —the Sermon on the Mount. The sun was streaming in through the antique glass panel on the front door. The brass candlesticks gleamed softly on either side of the marble table.

"Why haven't I noticed just how beautiful this little place is? It looks so pretty," I thought. "I hate to disturb the scene. I'll look for another Bible in the library."

I hesitated. I was held to the spot by the warm peace that surrounded me.

My eyes fell onto the open page. "How blest are the poor in spirit; the reign of God is theirs. Blest too are those who weep; they shall be comforted." Those words had power. (I had wept plenty in the last few years.) Now we were being comforted. Reverently, I folded the Bible shut and held it in my arms as I ran upstairs to get the hanging bag.

After our confessions, Monsignor Martin had assigned us both the same Bible readings —the first two chapters of the first letter of St. John. Frank wanted us to read them before we left on our trip. We sat together on the sofa in the living room of our home, and looked through the Bible until we found the first letter of John.

Frank began reading: "This is what we proclaim to you: what was from the beginning, what we have heard, what we have seen with our eyes, what we have looked upon and our hands have touched —we speak of the words of life."

Frank was impressed, "This is really the truth!"

He marked the place, shut the Bible, and gave me a hug.

By now, our patient little Beau was impatient, "What's taking so long? I will be starved by the time we get there."

He had mixed emotions. One of the biggest joys of his life was going to be with Gammie and Papa in New Orleans —not only that, his Uncle Will happened to be in from Virginia that weekend. On the other hand, he felt left out. We were going to the Bahamas without him.

Human nature is always resistant to change. Beau knew something big was going on, and he was not sure what it all meant. While driving to New Orleans, we began to talk about our very eventful day.

"Beau, wasn't the renewal ceremony nice? " I asked.

"I liked the wedding part, that was great, but I didn't like putting the rose on the altar. To me, it was a waste of a perfectly good rose. Daddy hardly ever gives you a rose, and then you go and leave it in church. I think that's dumb!"

A wave of guilt and regret swept through Frank. All of Beau's life he had tried to convince him that there was *no* God. Would Beau ever come to believe, too? He hoped it was not too late.

In his heart he prayed, "Dear Jesus, forgive me for denying You to Beau. Do something to help him overcome my bad example. Lead him to You, Lord."

Then, to Beau he said, "I didn't mind Mom leaving the rose in church. It was something we offered to God together."

"Well, it was *your* rose, but *I* never would have left it there."

The three story house on Palmer Avenue in New Orleans loomed large on the oak lined street. The servant's cottage behind the house had been our "nest" for four years. We belonged to New Orleans, too.

"Blow the horn, Daddy," Beau suggested happily. "If you don't they won't come running out to kiss us. I wonder what Gammie cooked?"

At the sound of the horn, a stream of family came running out.

"We didn't wait supper for y'all, but the redfish courtbouillon (a New Orleans specialty) is heating on the stove," Gammie said.

"Can I make y'all a drink?" Frank's Dad offered.

"How about some coffee, Dad. I'm drowsy from the drive." Frank said as he clasped his Dad's extended hand.

The next morning I was awake before the alarm clock went off. We were taking the earliest flight to Miami. I hurried up the stairs with a wake up cup of coffee for Frank, and gave him a big hug.

"Wake up, Babe, I want to be on that flight!"

"What time is it?" he asked opening his eyes.

"Time to give me a kiss. It's almost six. Let's get going."

Beau sat up drowsily as we hugged him good-bye, he gave us a giant squeeze.

"I'll be okay. I'm going to have fun here with Uncle Will and Gammie. I'll see you Sunday night."

"Be a good boy," I said, "I love you."

"I love y'all, too. Bring me a souvenir," he turned over and went back to sleep.

As the plane lifted off the ground, Frank squeezed my hand and bowed his head. I knew he was praying, I bowed my head and closed my eyes.

"Lord, please watch over us and keep us safe. Be with Beau, and don't let him be lonesome. Thank you, Lord, for this miracle. I can't believe this is us. Thank you, Lord, for how happy we are. Let us have a nice time. Our Father..."

Wow, it was wonderful to be able to pray. I *knew* the flight would be okay. All my worries eased away. We prayed again on the smaller plane that flew us from Miami to the Bahamas.

After we settled into our hotel room overlooking the sea, Frank told me, "When we were landing, the island looked so unimpressive, I was afraid you wouldn't like it."

"No way," I smiled and motioned him over to me, "this is perfect, the island is beautiful. I've waited ten years for us to go away together, just the two of us. This is a dream come true for me."

We knelt to pray. Prayer quickly became natural to us.

That evening after supper, instead of turning on the television set, we began to read the Gideon Bible that was in the hotel room. The stories, the parables, the psalms, sprang to life for us. We swam and sunned, dined, danced, and toured the island; but every spare moment found us reading the Bible. We literally could not put it down.

Splashing in the surf was washing out years of trouble and grief that had cluttered our lives. Reading the Bible led us to the discovery of a treasure of strength and faith.

On Friday morning we went out to the beach. Frank said, "I think I'll wear my glasses into the water. It's not too rough, and I won't go very far."

The sea was super salty and floating was a cinch. Frank, because of his glasses, stayed in water a little shallower than I did. I was floating on my back. I could feel the water beginning to get a little choppier, and stood up to see if the weather was clouding over. I looked for Frank. He was diving madly, up and down in the surf. The next time he stood up, I called out, "What's the matter?"

He was about ten yards away, and he said, "My glasses, I lost my glasses, how stupid of me to come in with my glasses!"

The water was very clear. It reached me to my chest and I could see my feet, but the waves had really picked up. There were white caps, small ones. As I watched him diving down again, I thought, "He'll never find them like that. This is going to mess things up for us. The rental car is already paid for —forty-eight hours. I bet he won't be able to read the Bible."

All of a sudden, I remembered our heavenly friend and matchmaker, St. Anthony. He was the patron of things lost.

We Find a Treasure

According to a sweet old nun I remembered, "All you have to do is ask St. Anthony to talk to Jesus about the thing you've lost, and Jesus will let St. Anthony help you find it."

Finding glasses in the sea was not easy, especially Frank's glasses. They had thin gold rims, not heavy dark ones. I closed my eyes. I thought of St. Anthony and of Jesus.

I prayed, "Tony, Tony, look around, something's lost and can't be found."

From this vantage point that rhyme sounds silly, and even sacrilegious, but that was the prayer I remembered from third grade. I was asking for heaven's help, it was simple and totally sincere. I opened my eyes and there at my feet, neatly folded, were Frank's glasses!! My heart skipped a beat. I was nearly bursting with joy —as much for the answered prayer, as for the recovered glasses.

Swimming over to where Frank was diving, the glasses held tightly in my hand, I called out, grinning from ear to ear, "Frank, Frank, I've got your glasses."

He was overcome with amazement, "Over there? Impossible —but how?"

I took a deep breath and said serenely, "I prayed. I closed my eyes and I prayed, and when I opened them, there they were!! They were neatly folded at my feet."

We held each other, it was a solemn moment. Once again the grandeur of God held us in hushed silence. We learned together just what kind of God we gave ourselves to — a loving Father. Our God took an interest in the smallest details of our lives. He didn't want our beautiful time together to be spoiled. He wanted Frank to have his glasses. That day we unashamedly said our grace before meals in the restaurant.

Sunday morning, a taxi took us to the nearest Catholic Church. We sat in the second pew. Scattered about in the congregation were fellow tourists from the hotel. We were caught up in the celebration from the opening prayer. The mass was a banquet welcoming me home like the prodigal son. "Lord," I thought, "How could I have stayed away so long?"

The rousing sermon touched me deeply. At first, tears welled up in my eyes; then they streamed down my face.

"Do you have a handkerchief?" I whispered to Frank.

He squeezed my hand as he handed me the handkerchief.

Before I knew it, I was stifling sobs. What must the celebrant have thought, to see this sobbing young woman in the second pew? I don't remember the whole sermon, but I do remember the priest asking, "Why do people find it so difficult to believe in the love of God?"

"We believe in all kinds of things, we believe in man's ability to travel in space, why don't we believe in the saving grace and boundless love of our heavenly Father?"

A hymn from my childhood came into my mind, "Oh Lord, I am not worthy." I certainly was not worthy, but Jesus *was* present and He invited me to His table in the Eucharist.

That afternoon, running and laughing, we made it to the plane as the engines revved up. We were the last ones to board the small aircraft to Miami. Four wonderful days had flown by. We left the island with far more than we brought to it. We decided to buy our *own* Bible the very next day. We decided to pray together, say grace before meals, and we had a beautiful story of God's love to tell Beau —the glasses.

We were in love. We were honeymooners, only in our case, there were three of us on this honeymoon —Frank and I, AND GOD!!

The next day we both went back to work. I gave notice that day, I would be leaving the minute they could find someone to replace me! I thoroughly enjoyed my job, but I knew that right now, the best thing for my marriage was for me to stay home and be a homemaker. It was well worth a try.

Frank and I met for lunch. Then at the rectory, Frank bought us each a pocket New Testament for our offices, and one for the car. We bought a St. Joseph Edition of the New American Bible for our home.

Frank suggested, "Let's go into church and read something. I have fifteen minutes before I have to get back."

"Sure, that's fine with me," I said. "Bill, the architect, had to cancel his appointment with me this afternoon. I don't have to be back until two."

The architect involved in the housing program I was directing, had occasionally mentioned his faith. Before I met Jesus, I had simply ignored his efforts to share his faith with me. Bill and his wife, Cheryl were members of the Abba Charismatic Prayer Community that met every week in the St. Mary Magdalen Community Center. They were part of a "prayer chain" that dedicated itself to the community's prayer needs.

Monsignor Martin had called the prayer chain the night of Frank's conversion. "Please pray for a couple that is turning to the Lord. Call the list, God is moving rapidly in their lives." That request was passed on. Fervent and faithful, God's servants stood in the gap for us, spiritually storming heaven with their prayers.

Monsignor Martin befriended us. We enjoyed our visits with him. He kept mentioning the prayer meetings and inviting us. He supplied us with volumes of books, which we devoured. But the majority of our reading was in our new Bible. We read it *constantly*. It was wonderful to discover the strength for our lives that came from reading aloud to each other in the evenings. Beau began to join us with some interest.

Go! You Are Sent 82

Frank read through the entire New Testament in his free moments. He finished it in *five days*! The rectory ran out of New testaments as he bought dozens more and brought them to the top floor of the courthouse, the jail. The Bibles were then distributed to the prisoners. Frank was a new man. His co-workers noticed it and commented on it.

He says people stopped him on the street or in the court house asking, "What's happened to you?" and "You look great, Mr. Summers, are you taking some new vitamins or something?"

Our lives were different. I often say it was like an interior decorator came in and did everything over. There were some struggles, but the victory was ours —new life and new values. A marriage "on the rocks" was now built on solid rock.

A couple of weeks after we got back from the Bahamas, Louise and her husband, Albert, invited us over for dinner. Almost as soon as we walked through the door, Albert said, "Man, y'all look terrific! What happened to the two of you? Maybe Louise and I should take a trip to the Bahamas."

Louise's eyes lit up. "What are you drinking?" she asked. "Genie, you come with me." In the kitchen, we hugged.

She poured our drinks and said, "Tell me everything! I want to hear every detail. Father Martin told me a little. but I want to hear you tell it."

"Louise, it's unbelievable the difference in our house. Jesus has come into our lives and changed everything."

Louise was visibly moved.

I continued, "I never thought it possible, but we really don't argue. We pray together, we read the Bible, we go to church. We renewed our marriage vows and everything. We're like newlyweds, after ten years! It's just amazing."

Louise put the cocktail napkins on the tray.

We rejoined the men in the library with the drinks. Even tonight's drinks were a departure from our former favorites. No "Scotch-on-the-rocks" for Frank, and no Martini for me —instead, we each had a simple glass of wine.

Albert's comment about the Bahamas had opened the door for us to tell him all about our experience with Jesus. He was skeptical. It was all so new to him. Our faith grew as we tried to explain it, that is the thing about the treasure of faith, the more you try to share it, the more you give it away, the more you get back. It is an unfailing wealth, more precious than gold.

Chapter Nine

More Freedom

"Let's go to some of those prayer meetings. You know, the Charismatic ones. Father Martin said there is a meeting every Wednesday night in the Community Center. They must be pretty good, cars are lined up everywhere." I asked Frank after our family prayers one evening.

"Why don't you go without me? I'll be uncomfortable there." Frank was decisive.

Friends and acquaintances had supplied us with books. Spirit-filled books were like manna from heaven for me. Some, we read aloud as a family. Most of the books were circulating in the Catholic Charismatic Renewal. I quickly developed a lively interest in this exciting movement in the Church. I was a little bit disappointed that Frank didn't share my interest. But I was happy with our life together.

"I prefer to be home with you than to go and miss out on our time together," I cuddled up to him.

"I enjoy our family prayers, too. But, if you want to go, please do," he said.

"Besides, I read recently that in the *Holy Spirit* we should 'Wait for the right time.' Frank, when it is *your* right time, it will be *my* right time, I said."

That right time was waiting for a series of events to signal its coming.

Louise arranged an interview for me with the former associate pastor who had written the article, *Wildfire in South-*

west Louisiana. He was newly assigned to a parish in Youngsville, a little town nearby. Many of the books I had been reading dealt with the healing power of the Holy Spirit. The purpose of the interview was to seek healing for my nephew, Bruce and Liz's child, now five years old.

Doctors had predicted Michael would live no more than six weeks. Yet, he lived to be a great blessing for all who knew him. He was severely handicapped, but just to be in the room with him was being near to love in its purest form. I called him my "Fat Pretty." Although he couldn't talk, I felt like he knew me. I desperately wanted him to be healed, and the Holy Spirit was using Father for physical healing in a mighty way. When he prayed, many were healed.

In the first part of our interview, I talked excitedly about my recent conversion.

He surprised me by saying, "In Abbeville, every time I gave Holy Communion to your mother, I would ask the Lord, 'When are you going to touch her daughter, Lord Jesus?' Exciting things are going on in the church these days, including healing, but not limited to it. Conversion, people finding their lives changed is probably the most exciting thing happening. Every week the number of people attending our prayer meeting is growing. Why don't you and Frank come?"

"Father, I don't want to force anything. When he comes, I want it to be because he wants to come," I answered.

"Can I pray with you? You mentioned that you wanted to know more about the Baptism in the Holy Spirit."

"Sure," I said, "What must I do?"

He walked over and knelt on the floor beside my chair. He held one hand uplifted to heaven and the other he placed gently on my shoulder.

"Just close your eyes and think of Jesus."

Go! You Are Sent

I closed my eyes and could feel the nearness of Jesus.

"In your heart, follow the prayer that I will pray— 'Dear Lord, Jesus, we come in your name. We ask, Lord, that you send your Holy Spirit to descend upon Genie and fill her with the fire of your love...'"

From above me I felt a warm and powerful presence. I began to feel that presence filling me —from the top of my head slowly to the soles of my feet. I felt entirely and completely secure and at peace. I had already begun to love Jesus, now I felt very much at one with Him. He loved me. He lived in me. From that moment on, I have never ceased to find in prayer that wonderful fellowship with the Lord and His Holy Spirit. In that moment, I would have been content to remain seated in God's presence forever.

Driving home, Louise told me, "In November there's going to be a Charismatic Conference in Lafayette. Speakers from all over the country will be there. Just imagine, thousands of people praising the Lord."

"When in November?" I asked.

"Thanksgiving weekend, at the Municipal Auditorium," she answered.

I sighed, "Well, I guess that's definitely out for us. That's the first weekend of duck hunting season. It would take a *super miracle* for us to get there."

"It seems to me that the Lord is doing miracles for you all the time," she laughed.

I smiled, "That's true, I'll have to start praying now, though."

Later that evening, as Frank and I shared the events of the day. I told him about my visit with Father Chachere. I explained the prayer for the filling of the Holy Spirit.

"Are you saying that something supernatural happened to you?" he asked in his "lawyer's voice."

I was totally unintimidated. "Yes, it was supernatural, it was the *power* of the Holy Spirit. I still feel Him with me now. I wish everyone could feel this way."

At every opportunity, Frank and I had been witnessing to Beau, talking about the gospel. His skepticism faded away as he realized that Frank and I were in love again, our home life had turned around completely.

The Holy Spirit called Beau through signs of His presence. One day, I was putting the food in the refrigerator, and telling him about the prayer for the Baptism in the Holy Spirit. "Mom", he said in a whisper, "While you are talking, there is a bright light around you."

My grandmother, Etta, had married again after the death of my grandfather. Her second husband, Mr. R. G. Garland, was a Baptist. He died in October of 1973.

Frank, Beau, and I joined the Gremillion clan at the funeral. That was our first Baptist service. The preaching was based on God's word and very powerful. We were inspired and consoled. On the way home from the funeral, Frank commented, "I could sit and listen to preaching like that all the time. Why are Sunday Mass sermons so short?"

"Most people want to get in and out of church on Sunday in an hour. Very few would be happy with a forty-five minute homily. *But*, they say that the preaching at the Charismatic Prayer Meetings is great. Everything they do is based on the Word of God. Can't we go, just once or twice?"

"When and where are these prayer meetings?"

"Tonight in Youngsville there is one. We could go home the back way and stay for the meeting," I said. (In my heart I was pleading with Jesus to make it possible).

Go! You Are Sent 88

"Well, we will drive though Youngsville. *If* the meeting is tonight, and *if* we get there right on time, I'll go; but I'm not going to wait around for a couple of hours," Frank asserted as we pulled into a shopping center in Lafayette.

I waited in the car while he and Beau went in to look for some hunting equipment. He bought a camouflage cover for his deer hunting bow. It seemed to take forever, and I really didn't have any idea what time the prayer meeting was in Youngsville. I just knew it was on Tuesday night.

I was slightly peeved as I thought, "He won't wait for the prayer meeting to start, but he'll sit for hours in a tree waiting for a deer to walk by."

I should not have fretted, the Lord's ways are above our ways. I asked Him to take charge of the situation and He did.

"Suppose we can't find the rectory?" Beau asked.

"We will."

As I prayed, I felt confident in the Holy Spirit, and joy welled up inside of me. From the Lafayette highway, we entered Youngsville and drove straight to the front door of the church. People filed into the rectory for the prayer meeting.

I couldn't conceal my excitement. I said, "We're exactly on time, it must start at seven."

"Let's park, Daddy. I think we were meant to be here," Beau said.

"I guess this is God's plan, for sure, I didn't plan it this way." Frank put his arm around my shoulder and our little family attended our first prayer meeting together. I introduced Frank to Father Chachere, and lots of other people welcomed us enthusiastically. We sat toward the back of the room in about the third to the last row of folding chairs. More and more people came in and filled the room.

Both Frank and I thought in silence, "We can't get out of here if we try."

They sang gloriously, and I began to sense very strongly the power of the Holy Spirit. It reminded me strangely of the Bayou Sale service. Then the praising started; I was unprepared for that much enthusiasm and volume. I wanted to abandon myself to it, but found, much to my surprise, that I was uncomfortable. Feeling uncomfortable myself, I wondered what Frank was thinking and feeling.

The young couple in back of us were saying "Praise you Jesus. Oh, Precious Jesus. Sweet Jesus. I love you, Jesus."

I couldn't help wondering if Jesus liked being called "precious."

Frank says that at first he felt so uncomfortable, he imagined himself offending God by being there. As he closed his eyes and bowed his head, he prayed. "Lord, please forgive me for being here. I'm sorry that I came, but I can't leave. I'm blocked in."

"Be quiet, Frank! These are *my* people. *I* brought you here. I have something to teach you tonight." The Lord's answer was crystal clear.

Frank relaxed. The priest moved down the aisles laying hands on those present. Frank felt, in the imposition of the hands, the same Holy Spirit he had been experiencing since the night of his conversion. He also felt reassured that God was there, touching all of those people with that same loving presence. When the meeting was over, we stayed for coffee and cookies in the kitchen of the rectory.

"Well, how did you like the prayer meeting?" our architect friend asked.

"I enjoyed the preaching and the sharing from the Word of God," Frank answered.

"What about the praising? What did you think of that?" he continued.

"Well, the Psalms talk about praising the Lord. It was a little livelier than I expected. But at the end, I really got into it," I told him.

A radiantly happy lady walked over to Frank and said, "The Lord must need someone to work for the poor."

He laughed, "He probably does."

As Frank introduced me, he reminded me of the census lady who had visited him right before our conversion. "God has worked wonders in our lives in these two months," Frank happily reported to her.

"I left your house praying for you, Frank, to find the Lord and to work with the poor," she beamed.

Still, time passed and Frank didn't hear the Lord calling us to attend regularly. There was more mountain moving work He had to do in us in the privacy of our home.

We were living a Spirit-filled and Spirit-led life as a family. The music group at Mass on Sunday inspired us to try singing in our family prayers. I borrowed an old Methodist hymnal from Louise.

Later, we looked through the hymnal to see which songs we recognized. The only song we all knew was, "God Bless America." Somewhat discouraged, I returned the song book to Louise and said, "All we know in here are the patriotic songs. Do you think Father Martin would let us take one of the song books out of the church?"

"I think the prayer group has them, and probably some extras. I'll ask them," she offered.

At night we established the practice of reading the Bible together aloud. We were willing to hear God speak to us, to lead us and guide us through the Scriptures. When Frank came across a truth that especially touched on my weaknesses, he emphasized it by the tone of his voice. I did the same. Our relationship no longer depended on either of us being "right." It wasn't choosing between doing things "my way" or "his way" —we were discovering Jesus' way and *His way* was always right.

One night, we were reading in Ephesians 5:

Submit yourselves to one another. Wives should be submissive to their husbands as if to the Lord, because the husband is head of his wife just as Christ is head of his body the Church, as well as its savior. As the Church submits to Christ, so wives should submit to their husbands in everything.

My Women's Lib past came rushing up to the surface. I could feel rebellion rising up in me, at the phrasing of the passage. It seemed so unfair. And yet, as we read the whole passage, the instructions for a husband were pretty tough, too. God's word demanded that he love his wife as Christ loves the Church. Well, Christ died for the Church, that's not holding anything back. It certainly requires that the wife be totally loved. The husband must think of her needs and be willing to meet those needs day in and day out. He can't be bitter about his role of loving service.

"I can't believe that teaching applies today, Frank. How in the world can you submit in everything?! Surely there's a more modern interpretation of these verses."

"Hey, wait a minute, don't get upset with me," Frank replied. "This is God's word, not mine. Just the other day, didn't you tell me that you felt the Lord was showing you that the whole of God's word is true. Remember, you said if some of it is true, and works in practical application, then all of it is true!"

Go! You Are Sent   **92**

I felt so disturbed, I hadn't experienced this irritation, this rebellion, in our almost two months of conversion. Frank could see I was sincerely struggling, he leaned over and gave me a hug.

"You like the part about 'Love your wives' don't you?" he teased.

I sighed and snuggled close, but I thought, "Tomorrow I'm going to talk to the priest about this."

I woke up at six in the morning to attend a week-day Mass. When Father Groth walked onto the altar, I thought, "Oh good, it's the young priest. He'll have the latest thinking on this issue of submission." After Mass, I approached him.

"Father, could I speak to you a minute?" I asked.

"Sure, come right on in to my office. Have a seat. What can I help you with?" he answered.

"I don't think we've met, I'm Genie Summers. My husband and I have recently come back to the church after ten years of being away. We were on the point of separation and divorce, but, Praise God, we experienced a real miracle in our relationship."

"That's fantastic! It sounds like y'all are on the right road for sure," he interjected with a burst of enthusiasm.

"It *is* great. At first my son, Beau, found it hard to accept the Lord, but we've been praying together and now he's coming to know Jesus, too. It seems to me we couldn't *have* a better family life."

"Wonderful, but what's the problem? Is something bothering you?" he asked.

"Well, yes there is. I don't know really how to express it."

"Just come right out and say it, I'm here to help."

"You see, Father, last night we read a Bible passage about wives having to submit to their husbands. It seems to me that those passages were meant for the Jewish culture two thousand years ago. They certainly can't be practical or applicable in today's society."

I'll never forget the big grin he flashed me as he said, "Let me tell you, *Sha* ('Sha' is Cajun French for *Cher* or Dear), those words on marriage in the Holy Scripture *are* for today. They are forever. God made marriage and HE knows how it works best. I'm counseling a lot of marriages, and in the ones where couples try to live God's word, God is healing hearts!"

For an instant, I couldn't believe my ears. Not only the words he spoke, but the utter conviction in his tone, assured me that Jesus was speaking through *him*. I flexed my spiritual muscle of faith to accept what he was saying, but as I did, I felt as though an enormous chain that held me bound was broken —dissolved. It was another case of "You shall know the truth, and the truth shall set you free." I was free —free to accept Frank's headship, free to submit to him as *unto the Lord*. It was a new tool for us, a formula for building our family life in God's plan.

I said simply, "Thank you, Father, thank you very much." I virtually floated out of the rectory and raced home to Frank.

Shortly after my visit with Father Groth, the Lord placed a copy of *Living Happily Ever After* by Bob Mumford in my hands. It fleshed out in print what He was trying to teach us. I was now convinced of my need to submit to Frank, and Jesus soon began to prove this word to me. One thing the Lord showed me was that submission was an attitude of the heart. In Proverbs 31, the ideal wife is described as an unfailing prize, more precious than pearls. I had to see myself as someone Frank could rely on *unfailingly*. When we prayed and discussed our

Go! You Are Sent 94

decisions, he could guide our family, knowing my heart was *unfailingly* with him.

He had some things to teach Frank about loving his wife, and laying down his life for me. Frank was a willing disciple.

We were going to a country club social. I had just finished reading the book. Frank came home from work late, only a half-hour before another couple would be picking us up. He went straight to the bar and fixed himself a Scotch-on-the-rocks. He hadn't done that very much at all since our conversion. It was typical, however, of how it used to be in our pre-Christian life. He usually had a few stiff drinks to prepare himself for this type of social occasion, which he found difficult for a variety of reasons.

We had lived and re-lived the same scene for ten years. He would fix the stiff drink. I would plead vigorously, "Frank, please don't drink on an empty stomach before we get there, you'll be smashed before the evening's half over."

"I can take care of myself, thank you," he would grumble, and off we went to the party, already angry with one another.

It had happened hundreds of times.

I was about to voice the usual complaint, when I remembered what I had read that very day about a wife's recourse to the saving power of God.

Instead of saying anything to Frank about the scotch, I screamed out to the Lord in my heart. "Lord, you know how I *hate* this drinking problem! I can't stand it when he gets 'tanked up' before we go out. But I'm not going to say anything. I'm going to be respectful and patient in this situation."

Frank brought his glass of scotch to the table where I was seated.

I felt the peace of the Lord, as I turned to Frank and asked in a sincere and gentle voice, "How was your day, today?"

More Freedom

He took his drink and pushed it away to the far edge of the table. He took me by both hands and pulled me to his lap. He hadn't done that since our first year of marriage. Tears welled in my eyes.

He spoke softly, "I had a very, very hard day. I barely had time to pray, I was so busy. We had over two hundred arraignments of criminals today. As usual, 'justice' isn't justice for everyone. The poor always get the short end of the stick."

I smoothed his hair and said, "I'm sorry you had such a rough day. If you're too tired, we can skip the party."

"No, we'll go. You're all dressed and they are probably on their way over here by now."

That drink stayed untouched on the other side of the table until I threw it away when we got home that night —sober and happy! That was the *last* time Frank ever came near a stiff drink. Jesus had made his Word good for me. I was impressed!

Our drinking to excess went by the wayside a little earlier than the smoking. One evening we went out with my brother and his wife, and Frank's sister and her husband, in New Orleans. We weren't drinking, but we each smoked about two packs of cigarettes in the course of the evening. The next morning, I woke up with my lungs squeaking and my mouth feeling like several dirty ashtrays.

"I really smoked too much last night," I said.

"Me too," he responded as he reached over to the bedside table and picked up the Bible to read. The two things didn't seem to go together —this cigarette hang-over and our prayer time.

"Why don't we give up smoking?" he suggested.

"I've tried so many times. I've often succeeded for two or three years, but I always go back to it," I answered.

Go! You Are Sent

He closed his eyes and prayed. "Lord, we want to quit smoking. You know how weak we are. We've tried before and failed. I know we can do it for Your sake, and with Your help. Please help us."

As he finished praying, I had an idea. "Why don't we figure out how much it would cost us to smoke from now until Christmas? Then we can give the money to some needy person as a sign and sacrifice to the Lord."

We figured out right away that it would be just about three hundred dollars. We dedicated three hundred dollars and found a miraculous freedom from all desire to smoke. The poor person we selected was able to have a bathtub installed in her home, and we were delivered from the habit of smoking. Praise God, we were free.

That donation was a kindergarten lesson about how a Christian should use money. Father Groth, about this time, was giving a series of sermons on time, talent and treasure. He spoke about tithing on Sunday at Mass.

As we climbed into the car, Beau asked, "How much money would we have to give to the poor, and to the church, if we tithed?" Frank is quick at math and had an answer for him in a moment.

Beau said, "Wow, Daddy, I think we ought to find a less expensive church or worship at home!"

We laughed 'til we cried, all of us. But we began tithing that very week. It was a first step in learning how to handle our money in the way the Lord would have us handle it.

We didn't even miss our tithe. Life had suddenly gotten less expensive. We didn't have a liquor bill. Our need for outside entertainment had diminished drastically. Our medical bills and drug store bills were minimal —the Lord was healing us, and keeping us well.

In one area after another, the Lord Himself was setting us free to change our hearts and our attitudes. We were free to trust Him in everything.

Chapter Ten

First Steps in His Service

The cool, crisp fall days beckoned us all to the farm. The farm was a haven to us. We spent all the time we could in the country.

"Frank, can we fix up the old tenant house on the farm as a camp?" I asked one day.

"I'm pretty sure it'll be fine with Mom and Dad. It's almost in ruins, we can only make it better."

Now, as a full time homemaker, I had time to devote to the project of cleaning up the dilapidated tenant house. Begging used furniture from Daddy, we furnished it sparsely, but cozily. We painted a few of the rooms, added some Dollar Store curtains, installed a pump for the water well, and "Voila," we had our camp.

Instead of stewing and fretting over Frank's hunting and fishing, I had decided to enter into his life. Beau and I spent the weekends there with him. Beau thrived on the great outdoors and began to hunt regularly with his Dad. The wild game from the morning's hunt would be cooked and waiting for the hunters as they came in from the evening hunt. Frank trained horses for us to ride. We fished in the canals, listened to Christian music and loved one another. There was so much peace.

Sacred to Louisiana's avid hunter is opening week-end of duck season. I resigned myself to the fact that the Thanksgiving

First Steps in His Service

week-end Charismatic Conference was a pipe dream for me. Almost resigned myself, that is, I hadn't stopped praying.

One day, Frank came home from the rectory. He was carrying a flyer about the Thanksgiving conference. "Do you think that Beau could stay at your parents house if we went to the Charismatic Conference?"

"Watch how fast I'll find out," I answered, unable to conceal my utter shock and amazement.

Speaking of utter shock and amazement, my Mom asked incredulously, "Does Frank remember that it's opening week-end?"

"Yes, and he wants to go anyway, Mom. Do you think you and Dad would like to come with us, I could find someone else to sit with Beau?"

"Not yet, Dad's not ready yet. I'll probably join you on Sunday afternoon, though," she said.

That Friday night, on the opening day of duck season, we sat at the conference.

"This is something else, I've never heard anything like it," I thought to myself as five thousand people around me sang the praises of God.

Our family had one more small miracle to add to its story. I knew that *only* God could have gotten Frank Summers smack dab in the middle of so many praising Cajuns.

Dr. David Duplessis, a powerful preacher called "Mr. Pentecost," gave the opening address. He had the whole attention of his audience as he told us "God has no grand-children." Dr. Duplessis emphasized a personal, close walk with Jesus that could stem from, but did not depend on, where our parents walked with Him. He called us to be a first generation of faith-filled Christians who would "Go" out to all the world with the Good News.

"That's a good sign, a Pentecostal preacher speaking at a Catholic Charismatic conference. God probably wants more interchange between churches," Frank remarked.

"I couldn't believe how well he knew the Bible!" I said.

"Yeah, he walked around with the Bible in his hand, but I never saw him read. I would love to know the scriptures that well."

"You're off to a great start, Frank" I said, "We've only been reading the Bible for three months, and we're halfway through already. That's a pretty good first step!"

By Saturday at noon, we had stood in the long cafeteria lines twice. The food was good, but we didn't know anyone well enough to join them at their tables. We decided to go to a nearby restaurant for lunch.

Walking through the parking lot, we halted as a friendly voice called out, "Where are y'all going?"

An energetic, hefty man sporting a crew cut flashed us a big grin. His smiling, small wife had a baby on her hip, and a toddler in tow. He asked with incredible friendliness, "How about having some lunch with us in our van? Diane makes the meanest fried turkey in town!"

As they caught up with us, we were warmly embraced. All this hugging was the normal way with these Christian brothers and sisters. It was genuine, and we responded with genuine hugging in return. Diane and I had been very close as children. Our mothers grew up practically as sisters, but I hadn't seen her in years. Both of us married early and had gone our separate ways. She looked beautiful, aglow in the Spirit, and hardly a day older than she had ten years ago.

"I'm Barry Bordelon, and this is my wife, Diane."

"Frank Summers, and my wife, Genie."

"Diane and I know each other," I said, "although it's been ages since we've seen one another. And who are these gorgeous little people?"

"This is Forest John and the baby is Elizabeth Ann," Diane smiled.

"What about lunch?" Barry asked.

I was surprised to hear Frank reply, "Are you sure there will be enough?"

We were hungry. (But more than that, we were hungry for someone to talk to about the Lord Jesus.)

"We've got six children," Diane said. "One thing we know how to do, is make food stretch."

We spent the rest of the conference with them. On the way back to Abbeville, Frank asked, "Are there any prayer meetings in Abbeville? We need this kind of input for our lives."

"There's one on Wednesday night, I've been wanting to go for a long time," I told him happily.

"Just remind me tomorrow morning, I'll put it on my calendar."

The next Wednesday, the parish community center filled up quickly. People came up to us to welcome us. A happy excitement filled the air, everyone was on fire from the conference. Our being there was a cause for rejoicing amongst many of our acquaintances, who had been praying for us for several months. Barry was in charge of the music ministry. We sang and praised! We praised and sang, and praised the Lord some more.

Every time I hear the song, "Psalm 89", that says "You give marvelous comrades to me", I'm reminded of the early days in the "Abba" prayer group. Frank and I couldn't get enough of sharing with others about Jesus. We arrived early and left last, talking 'til all hours of the night about the gospel. We were energized by God's power.

Jesus walked among us! He ministered to our needs. He spoke powerfully to us. He consoled us. He healed us. He exhorted us to holiness and to faithfulness through prophecy and visions. His Word spoken in the scriptures was like a two edged sword separating the bone from the marrow.

Beau always accompanied us and he recalls that "as the Holy Spirit came down upon the meeting, I'd be filled with 'side splitting' joy."

Frank's commitment was to do whatever the Lord would show him to do: keeping holy the Lord's day; tithing; the conference; and now a weekly prayer meeting where the fellowship with other brothers and sisters solidified our faith.

There was a lot of talk about building Christian Community like that of the early church. Our relationship with Barry and Diane snowballed. Together our hearts burned within us as we shared God's Word. They had six lively children and we had one. The kids loved one another. The Summers and the Bordelons went out to the farm together on the weekends. We planted a vegetable garden, but it was the fruit of the Holy Spirit that grew in our friendship.

The good news of our salvation was too good to keep to ourselves. We told everyone who would listen and even some who wouldn't. At times, Frank's clients telephoned him at home. When they couldn't reach him, many of them so needed to talk to someone that they would explain their legal cases to me.

Before I knew Jesus, I had to say to them, "I'm very sorry, I can't help you. I know nothing about the law. Please call back when Frank is at home."

First Steps in His Service

That situation changed. At last I had something helpful to say. I could tell them that there was no problem too big for the Lord to solve.

I remember the time when a lady called our house. She had the wrong number. I began witnessing to her, and in the end, she wept tears of joy as I prayed with her.

The "Abba" healing ministry met after each prayer meeting. Many people were healed. God honored our simple faith. The members of the ministry asked me to be the co-leader.

A young man who had been on tranquilizers for ten years was delivered from his addiction in one night. One woman worried about her mother who was too ill to attend the prayer meeting.

I felt inspired to tell her, "Have someone help your mother sit up on the side of the bed at 9:30 next Wednesday. We'll join her in prayer at the same time from here."

We prayed at nine-thirty after the prayer meeting. We all sensed the power of the Holy Spirit. I had a vision of Jesus at the mother's bedside, healing her.

"My mother sat on the side of her bed last week, and she felt a warmth run through her body at exactly nine-thirty. Praise the Lord, my Mama was healed!" the elated lady reported to the healing team later.

At a Charismatic Mass, Father Groth gave a teaching on the great commission. "Go, therefore into all the world and preach my gospel to every creature."

Early the next morning, Frank and I were in Father Groth's office, offering to serve the church in the church's ministry of evangelism. Actually, the church was just developing a ministry of evangelism.

Two nights a week we did our door-to-door evangelism through the the census. What an eye opener. People really

Go! You Are Sent 104

needed to hear about Jesus. It was a foundational step in our ministry as evangelists.

Sometimes their Cajun hospitality made it easy to invite our hosts into a deeper relationship with Jesus. Other times we encountered apathy and indifference. We had a few doors slammed in our faces, but Frank and I were not discouraged.

Many homes were dominated by a feeling of isolation and despair. The blaring of the television set contributed to the isolation. Frank didn't hesitate to reach over and turn off the set. That got their attention!

People were touched by our testimony. We prayed for their sick. We invited them to church. We could sense the excitement that comes in Evangelism. This was not *our* work. It was Jesus' work. He was doing it.

Frank and I always began in prayer, asking the Lord ahead of time to lead us to the people He wanted to talk to that night. Almost every time, there was evidence that the Lord had been preparing the occupants of the houses for our coming. He was doing great things in our hearts, too. We could go to complete strangers. Some were in our social category, and others were not. We learned how God's unconditional love reached out to everyone, in every circumstance!

Frank wanted to have his law work dedicated to the Lord. "I don't want Jesus to be an after hours sideline. I wonder if I should begin a prayer meeting in the District Attorney's office in the courthouse?"

"Lots of men would come, I bet," I said.

Every Monday, businessmen, clerical workers from the courthouse, and some professionals would give up their lunch hour to sing, praise, and worship the Lord. They shared from the scriptures. Their meeting was a sign of God in the midst of the work world.

Abbeville has two Catholic church parishes —St. Teresa of the Child Jesus, and St. Mary Magdalen. Father Floyd Calais, pastor of St. Teresa, worked closely with Barry and Diane. They were part of a team that gave the Pre-Cana instruction to prepare engaged couples for marriage.

The phone rang one afternoon; it was Barry. "Hey, Frank, I'm so excited. The couple that usually gives the Pre-Cana talk on *Order in the Family* can't be there tomorrow, in fact, they might have to drop out of the ministry altogether. I told Father Calais about y'all and he agreed that you'd be perfect for that talk. Can you do it?"

"Can we do it? What an opportunity. But, Barry, tomorrow? That's short notice. How can we prepare that quickly? How long does it have to be?"

"About an hour, and don't worry. The whole talk centers on what Jesus has been doing for you and Genie. You can share your testimony and some of the scriptures that brought your family into God's order," Barry told him.

"I only hope we can get something together."

"Look, Frank, we often stay up half the night talking about the need for people to be trained in the Lord's word on marriage —just talk on some of that stuff, you'll do fine. Let Genie give her testimony of how the Lord freed her, how she wants you to serve her as head of your home. Tell 'em how your life has changed, and don't forget to tell them to love their wives."

The ear piece of the telephone hadn't cooled off before Frank grabbed a yellow legal pad and his Bible. He sat in his chair with the Bible on his lap, writing away. I stood in the doorway watching him and smiling. How many times in our former life I'd wanted to be a part of his intensity.

Things were so different now. He included me in his work for the Lord. We were really one. God was the binding force of our love.

His voice interrupted my thoughts, "Babe, Barry said that you should give a testimony, too —about submission. I think you ought to work from a scripture. How about the one that you like so much from 1 Peter, Chapter Three?"

"Okay," I said, "let me get the supper on the table, and then, after we eat, I'll make some notes."

On the way to the Pre-Cana course we went by the Bordelon's. Every time we drove up to Barry and Diane's, a swarm of beautiful kids ran out to greet us. Beau loved staying with them while we went to meetings. Seeing the fun he had in the midst of the Bordelon kids, I realized how hard being an only child had been on him.

The other two couples on the team were Bill Bradshaw and his wife, Cheryl, and our long-time friends, Butch and Evelyn Hollier. Frank and I respected all the members of the team. They were living prayerful and Christ-centered lives. Not only that, we had a lot of good, happy fun. Father Waguespack, the assistant pastor at St. Teresa, was the team leader.

On the Pre-Cana team, we began to experience Christian fellowship at an even deeper level. The rewards of serving the Lord with others attracted us. We impacted those young couples in a life changing way. Frank's teaching evolved into preaching. The Word was being made flesh for us, as well as for the engaged couples. We couldn't preach what we weren't living. Pre-Cana ministry was a solid step in God's plan for the Summers family.

The core group of the "Abba" prayer group had fine leaders who diligently sought the Will of God. Vince and Kay Listi radiated confident faith. They had been childless for five years.

Doctors disparaged their chances of having children. The experts were wrong. The Abba Prayer Group and others prayed unceasingly for a Listi baby. As the gynecologists discovered each new obstacle, the Lord Jesus would remove it. Andrea Listi, and her four brothers and sisters, are living proof of God's power. Early on, God placed the Summers and the Listi family together for His service.

Frank and Barry talked to Vince and others whom they knew had a strong desire to build Christian community. We loved the idea of living in daily contact with those who loved Jesus the way we did.

"Diane, it looks like we're going to gather a group of those interested in living the community life. Frank suggested our camp at the farm. The only thing that worries me is supervising all those kids. We'll have to warn them about roaming off into the woods or the canals," I said.

"I told Barry that Sunday afternoon would be okay. I think the Listis already meet with some of the others on Sundays. We can go early and help get ready," she said.

Those Sunday afternoons out at Forked Island were extraordinary in some ways. Each family brought a picnic lunch out to the formerly abandoned tenant house. Seven couples and their children regularly attended. From time to time, single men and women and widows joined us. Occasionally one of the priests from the renewal came along.

The Lord spoke clearly to us —leading us on. The fellowship was sweet and exciting. The fire of the Holy Spirit fell on that little camp in the late Winter and early Spring of 1974.

We all wanted community. We all wanted community with each other. We wanted deep commitment. What would it take for us to be able to "share all things in common?" Frank and I, and Barry and Diane had been praying together a lot —really

Go! You Are Sent 108

seeking. It seemed to us that the Lord was serious. He called us to total abandonment.

In our private family life, Frank and I read the Scriptures and the lives of the saints, especially St. Francis. We sensed the Lord speaking to us about the invitation of the gospel to a Holy Poverty. As Frank shared our private guidance, the Sunday afternoon group seriously discussed the possibility of all of us selling our present homes and moving into some abandoned homes in a poorer section of Abbeville. Of course, the homes would have to be made livable. Two of the men in the group were architects, they even drew up plans for the renovation and restoration of the houses.

The actual blueprints were drawn before we had confirmation that the Lord would make these houses available to us. Thinking about being next door neighbors in the infancy stages of a community was very enticing. There were eight of these houses and seven couples —the eighth house would be the community center and maybe a common kitchen.

Suddenly, around Easter, our plans seemed to get bogged down in disagreement.

"These houses could be made into little jewels," one builder offered.

"What about the simple life? Aren't we trying to live gospel poverty?" I asked.

"Well, what about the scripture in 1 Timothy that says, 'Tell those who are rich in this world's goods not to be proud, and not to rely on so uncertain a thing as wealth.' St. Paul isn't telling them to be poor. I was poor all my young life. Furthermore, I believe that God provides us with the good things," another lady said, on the verge of tears.

The expression, "Back to the drawing board," usually means starting over to clear up a problem. Perhaps *our* problem was that we got to the drawing board *too soon*. Instead of focusing on the Lord in one another, we were focusing on the details of our future life together.

The Sunday of the this little incident, after everyone else drove away, Frank and Beau and I stayed on at the camp. We sat on the sofa, hand in hand.

"What *is* the Lord asking of us, the Summers?" Frank asked us. He pressed my hand and pulled Beau to him. "I believe we are ready to do whatever he shows us. We just need to be clear about what it is he is saying."

"Daddy, why don't we sing 'Lead us on, Oh Lord'?"

"Before we do, I'd like to share a reading I got the other day in my prayer time," I said.

He who seeks only himself brings himself to ruin, whereas he who brings himself to nothing for me discovers who he is. (Matthew 10:30)

"All those years I was going through an identity crisis, I was seeking only myself. But now that I've put all my hope in the Lord, not trying to *be* something or someone important, I'm discovering who I am. This really helped me.

"I'm happy to be me —Genie Summers, daughter of God, wife of Frank, mother of Beau. I've got an impressive identity."

"I like that scripture, Genie." Frank smiled, and added pensively, "What do you think the Lord might be saying to us, as a family, through that reading?"

"Maybe He's saying that we have to give up all *our* plans, all of *our* dreams, and He will show us who we are in *His plan*," was Beau's wise response.

"Good, Son. Let's ask the Lord to help us do that!" Frank said with a determined strength.

Go! You Are Sent

Frank bowed his head, "Lord God, Heavenly Father, You know how much we've grown to hope in building this community. We want to serve You with our brothers and sisters, to receive their love and to give them ours. But, if this is not Your plan, or if we're going about it in the wrong way, we surrender to Your plan and Your way. Please, lead us and guide us, Jesus. Teach us to serve You more perfectly. I want to fall into bed at night exhausted in Your service. Let us serve you in humble obscurity, just show us our identity. Wherever we fit into Your plan, Lord, that's where we want to be. Amen."

I kind of shuddered at the part about being exhausted in the service of the Lord, but the rest of the prayer really clicked in my spirit. In our walk with Jesus these eight months, serving Him had been our greatest joy.

Hadn't we seen the Lord use us constantly? The list of ways began to run through my head: evangelizing people in their homes through the census; participating in the Pre-Cana ministry; serving the poor in the St. Vincent de Paul Society; hosting our brothers and sisters in Christ in prayer for community; Frank reading at mass on Sunday; sharing our testimony with area prayer groups; the prayer meeting at the courthouse; leading the healing team; teaching Christian doctrine to young people; invitations to preach. This was only the beginning. We had taken solid first steps in His service.

I wondered, "How will He answer the prayer Frank just prayed?"

Enveloped in the presence of Almighty God, I knew instinctively that His answer would surprise and challenge us. I felt a small shudder of fear shoot through me, followed by a flutter of Holy anticipation.

Together we sang, "Lead us on, Oh Lord, lead us on!"

Chapter Eleven

Do Not Live in Fear, Little Flock

"Bye, Sweetheart, don't try to phone me, remember. To-day's Thursday. I'm going to have the telephone off the hook," I told Frank as he kissed me good-bye.

"What's Beau going to do if he needs something?" Frank asked.

"I told him to call Diane. He can walk to her house from school if he needs anything," I answered happily, thanking God that I had taken care of that.

In the early days of my spiritual pilgrimage, a whole day each week was dedicated as my prayer day. I prioritized Thursdays as the pivotal point of my schedule. In preparation, on Wednesdays, I cooked a double recipe of chile con carne or spaghetti casserole. Thursday, I minimized housework, searched the Scriptures, and visited with Jesus.

Psalm 40 was my favorite, I called it my "theme Psalm." I resonated with the words of the psalmist. The Lord had rescued me and put my feet upon a rock and steadied my steps. He put a new song into my mouth, and in His plans for me, there was none to equal Him. During a particularly tender moment with the Lord one Thursday morning in our living room, I felt His nearness and love.

I said to Him, "Jesus, I love you, I want to love you more. Everything I have is yours, everything I am is yours."

That day, Frank came home for lunch. As we ate our sandwiches, he reached across the table and took my hand.

"Today, while I prayed at the D. A.'s office, I heard the Lord tell me 'Sell all you have, give alms to the poor, and come and follow me.'" Frank's eyes steadily awaited my reaction.

"That's amazing," I answered doing my best to hide the bolts of thunder that were exploding in my head.

He squeezed my hand and continued, "Of course, we will decide this together, but I'm sure this is God's call. He wants us to do it."

Suddenly, I let out the breath that I was inadvertently holding.

"But how?" I was able to ask in a strained whisper.

"There are no guarantees. I'm not sure how this will all work out, or where God wants us to go from here," Frank shared.

"This is heavy. I can feel the presence of the Holy Spirit, though. I want to say 'Yes' but I'm afraid," I said lowering my eyes and staring at my half-eaten sandwich.

"I've given some thought how we could do it. I'll get a huge box. First, we'll go through the house and pick out everything we don't use, put those things in the box and sell them. Next, we'll go through the house and sell everything we don't absolutely need. Last, we'll sell everything else."

I was very near to being in a state of shock! The offer I made to the Lord, about an hour before, was echoing and thundering in my head.

"That's quick. Okay, Jesus, this is much too quick, I'm not ready for this," I thought.

Then, in very measured speech, I said to Frank. "I'm sorry, I don't think I can do it. Just this morning I offered God all I have, and I meant it, but now I don't think I can do it."

Frank's concerned face reflected the fear he saw in mine. I stood up and reached for the box of Kleenex.

"I didn't think He'd take me up on it so soon. Besides, your plan sounds like torture to me. It's like saying, 'we're going to cut off your arm, but just so you'll get used to the idea, we'll cut off the hand first, then the forearm and then we'll cut at the shoulder!'"

"That plan wasn't chiseled in granite. I thought it would be easier that way. Don't cry, Babe, is it the plan or the whole idea that upsets you most?" he asked.

"I'm not sure, both. Maybe your plan. I don't know," I answered trying to regain my composure and rationally look at what God was doing.

"It's okay, I understand. This will change our lives drastically," he said softly.

"If we pick up the brass cricket box on the coffee table, or the porcelain doves, every time I go in there, I'll see them missing, like a hole in my life. Even the things we nev..., nev..., *never* use have sentimental value for me," I said sobbing.

"Genie, I hate to leave you crying like this, but I have to get back to the office right away. Don't worry, though. I love you and the Lord loves you. He wouldn't call us to do something that He's not going to give us the grace to do. Tonight, when I get home, we'll pray for that grace."

"That's the trouble, right now I don't even want to pray for the grace," I sobbed.

He pulled out his handkerchief and wiped my tears, and kissed me longingly. He looked at his watch, and then rushed out the door. He had a very important pre-trial hearing.

I was absolutely miserable. I began to look around the house. We weren't super rich or anything, but we did have a lot of nice things. I starting trying to categorize them in my mind. I *used* my silver pitcher almost every night and my silver goblets regularly —where did they fit in the scheme? What

Go! You Are Sent 114

about our new upholstered furniture? I walked over to the new sofa and sat in the exact spot I had been sitting in earlier when I gave the Lord all I had.

Shutting my eyes, I said to Him, "Lord, I feel like the rich young man who went away sad, because he couldn't sell all he had to come to follow you. I'm surprised at how hard this is hitting me."

I sensed the Lord's presence. It felt as though I was kneeling at his feet with my head on his knees. "Remember, Genie, this is our day. You can say anything you like to me," I heard in my heart.

"All those lovely books You've been sending me about poverty and about St. Francis. And, yet, this still hurts. What about the house, Lord? It's not a rich house. It's just right for us. Besides, I never wanted to move again."

He heard me out. Jesus offered not His anger but His comfort.

"I'm so tired of packing up, I could scream! Jesus, you're going to have to send the Holy Spirit if you want me to pray for the grace to do this."

As I closed my prayer, I felt a tremendous peace. God is love, and love is patient and kind. I felt the Lord would be patient with me.

That night we did pray for the grace to embrace a life lived in Gospel poverty. We would be years learning about the pearl of great price, the pearl that you get when you sell all. For the moment, the pearl seemed terribly expensive. The Lord wasn't pushing me, and the head of our home wasn't either.

The first answer to the prayer for grace came with the absence of fear. "Perfect love casts out all fear." I wasn't ready to sell all, but at least I was able to think and talk about doing it.

Do Not Live in Fear, Little Flock

Two weeks later, was the annual Louisiana Lawyers Bar Association convention, in Biloxi, Mississippi. Our first convention since our conversion elicited mixed feelings. At past conventions, we spent the whole weekend partying. What were we going to do this time?

We witnessed so boldly in other circles, would we have the courage to stand for Jesus in this crowd of attorneys? Surprisingly, witnessing to our old friends came very easily. I guess we hadn't realized how obvious our profound change had been. They could see it in the way we related to each other. They knew something was different, because we weren't getting into the drinking scene at all.

Frank's dad sat as a Justice on the Supreme Court, so we had great accommodations in the suite adjoining theirs. Part of our plan for the long weekend was to spend quality time with his parents. They didn't really understand what had happened in our lives. It was a great time to be with them. Some workshops especially interested Frank for his work in the D.A.'s office. We enjoyed socializing with our friends over luncheons and dinners. One of our greatest hopes for that weekend was to get a little rest.

On the second afternoon of the convention, Frank took a nap. I decided to have my prayer time. Frank's proposal that we sell all, engulfed my thoughts. Hadn't I offered the Lord God everything? Obviously, the Holy Spirit was at work in this. In Biloxi, away from the house and our things, it was easier to come again to the Lord in total sincerity and honesty.

"Lord Jesus, I know you called the rich young man to sell all he had, I can understand why he couldn't. I can also understand why he went away sad. Was he just an isolated example, or did you call others to do the same thing? Show me clearly, Lord," I prayed.

Go! You Are Sent   116

God's presence surrounded me. I inhaled His love. I opened my bible and read:

> Do not live in fear, little flock. It has pleased your father to give you the kingdom. Sell what you have and give alms. Get purses for yourselves that do not wear out, a never failing treasure with the Lord which no thief comes near nor any moth destroys. Wherever your treasure lies, there your heart will be.   (Luke, Chapter 12, verse 32)

"Do not live in fear, little flock..."

I thought, "'Little flock,' this is a term of endearment. Jesus is speaking to someone he loves and is responsible for —he's offering them the best he can give —the kingdom of heaven, a never failing treasure! These aren't the words of someone who is trying to cramp the style of an unruly people.

I heard His unmistakable interior voice saying "Genie, you are one of my precious sheep. Have no fear!"

Excitement welled up within me.

I scanned further back in the reading. This talk of Jesus to His disciples took place in a crowd. The crowd He addressed had so many people that they were "treading" on one another. The rich young man hadn't been the only one who heard this message. Jesus spoke to all of His disciples, offering to us the kingdom and the treasure.

My whole heart and soul responded.

"I accept your offer of the kingdom and the treasure, Lord. I agree to sell all we have, including the house, and to come follow you. Where are we going, Lord? Please, prepare Beau. Give him courage and understanding," I said.

On the heels of my "Yes," an assurance, a Holy anticipation filled me.

"Frank, Frank, wake up. You told me we could take a walk on the beach to watch the sunset." I poked him gently.

I love sunsets, especially at the beach. I guess I'm an incurable romantic, too. My exciting news required a beautiful setting. The beach wasn't very crowded. The sky was completely overcast.

After we had walked awhile Frank said, "It doesn't look like there's going to be much of a sunset today, it's too overcast, do you want to go back in, or do you want to sit on that jetty over there for a while ?"

"Let's go sit over there, I have something I want to talk to you about," I answered.

I was disappointed about the sunset, but I knew my news would brighten the evening. We sat down. He put his arm around my shoulder.

I began, "This afternoon while you were sleeping, I had a wonderful prayer time. The Lord showed me that we are His precious little flock..."

Frank looked tenderly at me as I verbally surrendered our material possessions to the Lord. He could see that the Lord Jesus had enabled me to trade my possessions for the Kingdom of God.

I was happy with my decision, and it showed.

"Babe, I *knew* He'd give us the grace to answer His call to sell all! How long has it been since we began praying about this? Two weeks? That's fast."

"Fast? Maybe for you." I said. "These two weeks have absolutely dragged on for me. The challenge to say 'yes' was in my mind constantly. But *right now* I feel an overwhelming peace and, more than that, an excitement about what He has in store for us!"

It was time to be getting back. We had a dinner date in an hour. We walked hand in hand down the beach, the desire to see a beautiful sunset had slipped away unnoticed in the immensity of the moment.

But, after we walked about thirty yards down the beach, I heard the Lord tell me, "Genie, turn around."

I stopped.

I turned around.

I gasped with surprise. The whole, entire sky was turning the most glorious golden red I'd ever seen. A truly glorious sunset —it was His gift to me. His special kiss for His little lamb.

On the drive back to Abbeville from the convention, we made some logistical decisions. We decided to let my Daddy sell the house. He was a Realtor. We decided, too, that we wanted to do it quickly and make a clean break.

Sunday night, we drove straight over to Barry and Diane's to tell them our news.

"Yes, do it!" Barry beamed.

"What are y'all going to do first? Have a garage sale. I love garage sales. Barry and I can help." Diane suggested.

The Bordelons exuded enthusiastic support. Gospel poverty and this whole area of God's Word had been the subject of a quite a few of our late night discussions. Together we had explored the call Frank and I experienced. God had talked to us about a real poverty, a tangible poverty —not only detachment. Gospel poverty meant not destitution or desperation, but an entering into the heart of God with all we had, expecting from Him all we needed.

Beau had spent the night with the Bordelons. He listened in rapt attention to our story of the decision to sell all. His reaction mattered greatly. He had already read the entire New Testament and was working on the Old Testament.

Beau added his "Yes" to ours.

"Mom, what about my bike? There are some things that I still need. Are we going to sell my Hot Wheels collection?" he asked curiously.

"We'll go through your stuff together. God will show you what you need to keep," I answered, tussling his tow head.

Our plans took shape quickly and we easily made decisions as a family about our big step. First, we'd have a garage sale. The ad ran in the paper by Wednesday. Heirlooms went back to family members. My newlywed sister and her husband needed odds and ends, some of our furniture suited their needs. We'd move out to the camp at the farm and keep only the household goods most essential and serviceable, including the washer and dryer.

Living way out there, demanded that we keep the two cars for commuting. The Volvo was eight years old, and the Vega was new but not luxurious, and it was paid for. Yes, both of the television sets would go.

The little details of selling everything became a bit of a problem for us. If the Lord wanted us to give the money we made from the sale of our things to the poor in alms, then how should we do it? We had never read a book telling us how to go about *selling all* for Jesus.

"Frank, should we try to get the best price we can, so that the poor will have more money? That'll mean a lot of investigative work. I'll have to find out the going price for each item."

"Look, Genie, for our own sakes, let's do this as easily as possible. If we sell things as a bargain, they will sell quickly."

The day before we opened the garage sale, our families came over and bought some of the stuff that they thought we were selling at "give-away prices." Mom bought a set of Spode china that I purchased piece by piece in London.

Go! You Are Sent 120

"Just in case you come to your senses, it will be there for you." Mom teased.

Frank prayed, "Lord, please clean this place out, don't leave us with too many things hanging around. Send the people to whom these things will be most useful."

People had heard the news that we had completely "flipped out." On the day of the garage sale, they came in a steady stream all day, hunting bargains. In one day *everything* went!

The town was buzzing with speculation about our sanity. Friends dropped in during the days before the garage sale to advise me of the gossip and to convince me to reconsider.

Some of our Christian friends stayed completely away from us and the garage sale, because they didn't know how to react to us. A few told us later, they didn't want to take advantage of us in our radical zeal for the Lord. In the likely possibility that we changed our minds, they didn't want us to resent them for having bought our stuff.

Frank and I walked around the empty house after our garage sale and thanked God that it had been wonderful instead of painful. This day had been a spiritual coup for us. By God's grace, we had the ability to obey His call.

The Kingdom of God filled our empty house, the little flock of the Lord felt safe in His arms.

Chapter Twelve

The Vision

We moved out to the farm on May 11, 1974, on our eleventh wedding anniversary. Nine months before, we'd been on the verge of divorce. Now it seemed we were a whole lifetime away from that hideous threat to our family.

Beau suffered repercussions of the garage sale.

"Mom, I sold my toys and stuff because that's what I wanted to do. But the kids at school said that I did it because y'all forced me," he told me one afternoon shortly after we moved to the farm.

"Well, Beau, that's what Jesus warned us about —persecution."

"I don't mind persecution for me. But," he winced and continued, "I hate it when they say y'all are crazy."

"Are we crazy now, or were we crazy when we were about to get a divorce? Come give me a hug and we'll fry up some cinnamon doughnuts."

"Mommee told me something the other day that made me laugh," Beau said. "She said 'I prayed so hard for y'all. For ten years, I begged the Lord to bring your family back to church. Now I think I prayed too hard!'"

The sacrifices of living out in that poor tenant house taught us plenty. Gospel poverty was a privilege, a glimpse of heaven. All we needed was God. He gave us more than we asked for. The beauty of God's creation upheld us. There was a small lake in the back of the house, where we watched scores of

Go! You Are Sent	**122**

spectacular sunsets. Simplicity inspired prayer. Kingdom living captured my heart.

The prayer for community out at the farm had served a multitude of purposes in the life of the Summers family. We had grown in boldness and faith. We confidently manifested the charismatic gifts of the Holy Spirit. The guidance of God, in a personal inspired way, had brought us where angels fear to tread.

The families seeking community continued to meet as a group for another six to eight weeks after we moved out there. The eight houses on Hawthorne street never became available to our group. Slowly, we disbanded.

Frank had experienced most of the Charismatic gifts, except the gift of visions. In one of our group meetings, there were two or three visions that prompted the decision to lay aside the seeking of community at this time. Frank wondered, "How reliable is this gift of visions?"

He found some books on spiritual gifts, then got out the concordance. He carefully read and studied the scriptures in the Bible concerning visions. Through his study, he accepted wholeheartedly this gift, which both Beau and I were experiencing.

One Sunday evening, the group left, we ate dinner and Frank sensed that we should pray as a family. During this prayer, Frank had his first vision.

"I saw a faithful servant of God, who was completely worn out from life's struggle, walking the last stretch of life. As God's servant approached the glory of God and heaven, he died. And in death, he crossed into the luminous splendor. As the servant of God was engulfed in the splendor, God zipped up the vision, (like a purse zipping closed) and then it was gone," Frank explained.

"What do you think God was trying to show you by the zipper?" I asked him.

"I interpret the zipping to be the Lord's way of assuring me that the gift of visions is His gift. It is a picture representation of the Lord's word to us," Frank answered. "He can give visions when He wants to, and He closes them when we have gotten the message.

"The prophet Ezekiel saw the visions of God, that's how God taught him," Beau commented.

Beau went to bed at about eight thirty. Frank and I stayed up talking. I made coffee and while I was pouring it, Frank was praying. Suddenly, I could hear him enter into worship, softly and reverently.

"Praise you, Lord. Glory be to you, Lord, Oh Alleluia, Jesus!!"

I went to sit down next to him. Moving in closer, I began to feel the presence of God. God was manifesting Himself to us in such a strong way, that it was really frightening.

It was the first time I understood why, in the Bible, the angels always say to men, "Don't be afraid!"

The majestic power of His presence was in and of itself a clear message. We understood that He was saying, "I'm going to tell you something important! Pay attention!"

"I see another vision," Frank said. "In it, we are crossing the ocean. The Lord is sending us to some islands —tropical islands. He is showing some tropical flowers. Now I see some brown skinned people. There's a mission type building, maybe a hospital or school. I see lots of palm trees. He is showing the shape of the islands."

"Babe, go get a tablet and a pen and I'll draw the shape of the islands," he directed.

Go! You Are Sent 124

By now, there were goose bumps on my arms, and my breathing was measured. I found the tablet and pen. Frank drew the shape of one island with a little island off the tip of it. God's presence was still overpowering. We were like two little children. Our Father sat us down and spoke unhesitatingly to us.

Frank continued, "I think He wants to show me some more. You take the pen, and I'll tell you what He shows me. You can write it down."

The vision continued off and on for about an hour and a half. He showed Frank at least three different sea crossings. There were several scenes in each part, each scene distinct from the one before. There were pictures of us in service —Frank with his Bible open in his hand, sharing the word, and also of him distributing communion.

In the course of the vision, the Lord challenged us. He presented to us a variety of possible sufferings, trials and dangers. We understood that He was asking "You might meet up with a difficulty such as this, will you accept it and keep on serving me?"

We'd have a moment to say "yes" and then the vision would resume. An interview with God is a totally unforgettable experience.

Here was the answer to our prayer of abandonment, our offer to serve Him. After the vision closed, we talked and reflected until four o'clock in the morning. We were in awe of what had just happened. The Lord God had called us to be missionaries. Missionaries!

It was an exciting thought, and a frightening challenge. By now we were accustomed to the Lord's method of operation. We knew He often waited to give the grace of the assignment at the very last moment.

The thing that worried Frank the most, was the pragmatic carrying out of the vision.

"Should we get on a boat tomorrow morning and just take off?" He asked aloud.

"Is there a book on becoming missionaries? Who can we talk to? I wish we knew where to begin." I wondered too.

The next morning at the breakfast table, we shared with Beau what happened last night. He was impressed. He was thrilled. We asked him not to talk about it until we had a little better grip on what it meant, and on how we were going to start. Of course, he had the same reaction we did, a fear of leaving.

"What about leaving my grandparents? What about the Bordelons?"

"Son, I've never felt surer about God's will! He knows the difficulties involved. He knows how to take care of those we leave behind."

"That's right, Beau, we had no idea how wonderful it would be out here on the farm until we actually sold everything and moved," I said.

"Y'all just pray for me, okay," he said. "I'm ready to go, but, I like it out here on the farm. I hate to leave."

Frank had to be in court in Franklin, Louisiana, that day to represent the Southern Mutual Help Association. On the board of directors of S.M.H.A. was a priest. They went to a restaurant for lunch.

During the meal, Frank asked him, "Father, what order do you belong to, and does your order have anything to do with the missions?"

"Why sure, I'm a Marist, and we are a missionary order."

"Do y'all have any missions on islands?"

Go! You Are Sent 126

"Oceania (the islands of the South Pacific) is our principal mission field!"

"Do the Marists ever use lay people in their missions?"

Father thought a second, and answered, "I think so, but you could write to Father Paul, our provincial, and ask him. He would know a lot more about it."

We were eating a watermelon on the back porch, watching another sunset when Frank happily reported to us his conversation with the Marist priest.

"You're not serious, wow! I can hardly believe it, the islands of the Pacific! It sounds like the Lord is in a hurry," I said when Frank finished.

"Did you write to Father Paul yet, Daddy?" Beau asked.

"Yes, as soon as I got back to the office, I wrote a letter. Mom and I might go to the library tomorrow morning, to see what we can find out about the islands, and the missions.

That night, as we gathered in prayer, we held hands and sought the Lord. Frank sincerely implored God's help, "Jesus, we are already spiritually afloat in our little mission boat. Our boat feels like a canoe on the vast ocean. For us, the course is uncharted. Please, be our captain. Guide us safely to the place where we need to be. Amen."

A wave of peace, the peace that passes all understanding, buoyed us up when we asked Jesus to be at the helm of our "mission boat." We were not afraid.

Chapter Thirteen

Ready, Set, Go

Atlases, encyclopedias, National Geographic, reference books, and two legal pads full of citations and notes covered our library table. We'd been there for hours, nothing precisely fitting the vision had turned up.

"I never dreamed there were so many islands. Island nations, island territories, groups of islands we've never heard about. I don't think we're going to find our mission destination by library research, Babe," Frank leaned back and stretched.

"You're probably right, maybe we should try another tack," I answered.

"Let's look up Catholic organizations that use lay people in mission. We can write some letters."

Frank and I composed and mailed letters by the score. It was a long and tedious process. One office would refer us to another. The arduous search for an opportunity to serve tested our resolve. We learned that Catholic Lay Missionaries who wanted to tell the world about Jesus had to be dauntless. We were ready to go, but the Church was not ready to send.

Frank's arrival out at the farm with the mail, was the highlight of each day. Waiting for the "Go" signal after having made a decision was torture. Still we trusted in Jesus.

"This organization doesn't take children," Frank said plopping opened envelopes on the kitchen table.

"That's almost as hard to hear as the news that came in yesterday's mail. 'You are over-qualified and would be bored in our mission work,'" I complained.

"Hey, this is new. These people want us to take the Minnesota Multiphasic Personality Inventory." Frank handed me another manila envelope and smiled. "I wonder if Peter and Andrew had to take that test before they went out?"

Meanwhile, the Lord was working on other fronts in our lives. Because of the negative reaction in Abbeville when we sold all we had, we hoped the opportunity to serve in the missions would present itself, and then we'd just take off and go. Our plan was that Frank would resign his position and close his office. Then, we'd tell our families —all in as short a time span as possible. I guess we wanted to sort of "sneak" out when no one was looking.

The Lord had other plans. He began to speak to Frank. "If you are willing to serve me full time in a land far away, why not serve me full time right here in Abbeville?"

That was a very hard word for Frank to hear. The Law had been his life. Thinking of closing his practice and resigning his position made more sense if the mission plans were final.

Frank talked to his Savior, "What should I do while I wait, Lord? How can I be useful to you?"

The Lord kept saying, "Obey and trust!"

We had already shared our vision with Barry and Diane. The Bordelons felt God calling them to be in mission, but their hearts were led to the mission fields of New Mexico to work among the Navajo Indians.

While we waited, the Lord gave us a special gift. A retired missionary priest, Father George Pellegrin, was assigned to our church parish. Frank told him about our interest in missions. He encouraged us daily! He knew well the needs of

God's poor, many wait in darkness, to see the great light! He empathized with our zeal.

Father George had been in India. His eyes brimmed with tears when he reminisced about the beautiful people he had served. Beau's face glowed with anticipation of mission life as Father Pellegrin told stories of the tigers and cobras he met as he went out in the name of the Lord.

Our longing to go into mission increased, but the Lord made it clear that Frank was to give up being a lawyer and start serving Him full time right there at home. After discernment and prayer, Frank said "Yes, Lord. I'll give up the law and serve you full time here in Abbeville."

Frank handed in his resignation at the District Attorney's office. He called in his clients and referred them to his brother, Pres. Telling his Dad was very difficult.

The Abbeville Meridional was a traditional hometown newspaper. Back then, it put the obituary notices on the lower right hand corner of the front page. The Sunday that Frank's retirement from the D.A.'s office appeared in the paper, his picture and news article were placed in the exact spot where the obituaries belonged.

It was almost as though the Lord was saying, "This is it, Frank, you really are dying to yourself."

The article appeared on Christ the King Sunday. There was to be a big Christ the King rally at the Catholic school football stadium. We wanted to go, but just didn't have the courage to face all our friends and their questions about what we were going to do next, because we didn't have any answers.

Instead, we selected the quiet and anonymity of the church. We longed to spend an hour in prayer in honor of Christ the King. As soon as I knelt down and placed myself in God's presence, I began to weep.

Go! You Are Sent 130

"Lord Jesus," I cried "Why is this so hard? The uncertainty of the future weighs us down. Are we really crazy as others have said, or are we on the right track? What will we do now?"

All of a sudden, the church began to fill up with people! Most of our friends and acquaintances were there. The rally at the football stadium had been rained out. The church was the site selected as an alternative in the case of inclement weather.

I dried my eyes.

The animated singing filled the air and my spirits were lifted. Father Paul Metrejean, a former associate pastor in Abbeville, was the principal speaker. His homily that day was one of the greatest signs of God's faithfulness to us that I've ever experienced.

He preached with utter conviction, "The purpose of this rally is to proclaim that Christ is King, *but* is he really king of our lives? How many of you are willing, as some have, to sell everything, to give up your career to demonstrate that Jesus Christ is indeed the King of your life?"

He boldly proclaimed the need for total abandonment. Many people, despite themselves, turned around to look at us. We could hardly believe our ears. Jesus, our King, cared about our reputation. He knew our distress. Had we missed the rally, we would have missed this message of encouragement. God knew that. We had come to church. He sent the rain, and the rally came to us!

By God's leading, Father Floyd Calais had invited us to work full time in St. Therese Parish. He respected and admired our spiritual decisions, and knew his parish could use us as its servants. That invitation was also a sign that God wanted to keep us busy doing His work.

Father Calais asked Frank to preach the homily the day the Bordelons left for the Checkerboard missions. Our own call was further implanted in Frank's heart as the congregation listened to a hopeful missionary preach on the missions. They left a month or so before Christmas. We had Christmas at the farm that year, just the three of us. It was peaceful and a little lonely. The Bordelons were already sending happy reports of their mission to the Navajos.

The day after Christmas, we drove into Abbeville from the farm. Frank said "Let's check the mail. Then, we'll see if Father needs us."

Frank ran into the law office where we still received our mail. He came bouncing out of the office, waving a piece of paper. "This is a message that the secretary took the day before Christmas. It's from Father Paul, the Provincial of the Marist order, in Baltimore. He has a place for us to serve in mission."

"A place in the missions? That's our real Christmas present!" I exclaimed.

We drove straight out to Kisinoaks to use the phone. We didn't have one at the farm. Father Paul said on the telephone that there was an opening for a lay volunteer family to teach English and Religion in a Marist Catholic school in the Tonga Islands.

Father's first question was, "Are you willing to go?" His second question was, "Can you be ready to go in three weeks? School starts in Tonga the beginning of February."

It took us about thirty seconds to consult one another —we came up with a definite "Yes, we'll go."

When the news finally sank in, we nearly exploded with excitement.

"Praise the Lord, Frank. God is going to fulfill the vision."

"And not a moment too soon for me, either. I was beginning to think we were not on the right track or something," he said.

I asked Frank, "Where in the world is Tonga?"

Go! You Are Sent 132

"Father Paul said it is in the South Pacific near the Fiji Islands. He didn't seem to know all that much about it. He said he'd be coming in a week or two to talk with us and brief us on the mission."

"The Tonga Islands, did y'all find those in the library?" Beau asked.

"Wow, I can hardly believe it's finally happening. Where's our atlas?" I said, frantically searching through a stack of resource books we had in the car."

I found a travel book in my parents' library. The book gave a short description of this Island Kingdom. The article mentioned the beautiful wooden palace occupied by the past monarch, Queen Salote. There was a picture of her star-shaped outhouse. Each point of the star had a private privy.

I gulped a little as I read it, thinking "If the Queen has an outhouse, I wonder how we'll be set up."

It didn't really matter. The thought of the opportunity to bring the good news to the people at the ends of the earth refreshed us. Our three weeks of preparation raced by. It was hard to break the news to our parents, but our enthusiasm knew no bounds.

St. Therese Church Parish celebrated a beautiful commissioning Mass for us. We were presented with our mission crosses by the Marists. Father Calais gave a meaningful, rousing sermon. The church was packed with family, many fellow Christians, and well wishers.

Afterward, at Kisinoaks, Mom and Dad prepared a roasted pig with all the trimmings for a Cajun send-off. I walked along the Bayou for a last, loving look. The winter wind whistled through the leafless trees. Louisiana bid us adieu. The glory of God smiled upon us.

Ready, Set, Go

Our first mission flight to Tonga laid over in Los Angeles and as our jet left the orange skies behind us, we grasped hands and prayed. "Father in heaven, again we offer ourselves to you in service of the gospel. Make us worthy of this great privilege. Let our lives, even as we travel, give testimony to you. Jesus, we are your humble servants. Send the Holy Spirit upon us to enliven our zeal. Train us, Lord, in mission life. Prepare a place for us, not only to make a home, but a place for us in the hearts of the Tongan people. Amen."

Frank had barely ceased praying, when the thought occurred to me and I whispered to Beau, "The people on this flight are blessed to be traveling with us."

"Your humility is monumental, Mom," he laughed.

"It's just that I am absolutely sure we'll make it to Hawaii. God is sending us. He'll get us there."

We spent three days in Hawaii as the guests of the Marists. They had a large parish on the main island called Star of the Sea. We basked in the tropical climate, rested, and prayed. The Lord knew we needed those few days of rest. Beau enjoyed the fellowship with the priests and wandered around discovering new tropical trees to climb.

We asked the priests about Tonga, had they been there? They described it as a small, peaceful, group of islands, basically flat land, covered with palm trees and surrounded by beaches. Then they said, "Wait until you hear the singing in Tonga. They sing like angels. There's nothing quite like it."

Frank recognized in Hawaii some tropical flowers he had seen in his vision; God's word was being fulfilled. Being a part of the Marist volunteers and knowing that they were dedicated to the Blessed Mother helped us see the role the Lord wanted a devotion to Mary to play in our lives. She was our model for

Go! You Are Sent

"Doing whatever He tells you." Her "yes" was the first acceptance of the good news. We needed her example.

The next stop in our ten day journey from Abbeville, Louisiana to Tonga was Nandi, Fiji. We were exhilarated as we drove along the narrow road to a small rectory where we would be guests for the night. This was a lot less American than Hawaii. Men, clad only in shorts, climbed palm trees to get coconuts. They did it with such ease and grace.

Beau (ten years old) said, "I hope I can learn to do that."

The priest, our host, laughed. "It's not as easy as you think."

The next day we were back at the Nandi airport, a couple of hours early. We had to take a smaller plane to Suva, the capital of the Fiji Islands and our connection point for Tonga. We checked in our luggage and bid good-bye to our host, who hurried back to say a mass for the school children.

The airport had a very small coffee shop. We decided to wait there for our flight. Among the few occupants was a priest and one other man having a snack.

I did a double take, "Frank, that man in the coffee shop is Ralph Martin, from the Word of God community in Ann Arbor. He was one of the first people at Dusquene to be baptized in the Holy Spirit. He gives teachings at Conferences. I remember seeing him in the film they showed at the Charismatic Conference in Lafayette on the Word of God Community"

"Come on, Genie, you can't be sure."

"I am sure! He's one of the co-ordinators of that community. He was on the film a lot. He has wonderful eyes."

We walked over and introduced ourselves. It was Ralph Martin and a priest from Ireland who was serving in Nandi. They invited us to join them.

Ready, Set, Go

"We're on our way to Tonga to live in Mission," Frank told them our story.

Ralph was returning to the United States after a trip to Australia to help establish a Charismatic Covenant Community there. Nandi was a planned stop. Archbishop Pearce of Fiji had scheduled Ralph to speak at the conclusion of a retreat for priests, seminarians and religious sisters from throughout that region of the South Pacific.

"The Archbishop has asked me to introduce the Charismatic Renewal and then conduct a session of prayer for the Baptism in the Holy Spirit," Ralph told us. "Maybe you can join me in that ministry."

"Thanks, we'd love to. Father LaBreque is meeting us at the airport in Suva. Perhaps he can take us to the Retreat facility," Frank accepted the invitation with pleasure.

A beautiful circular rainbow glistened against the clouds below us as we flew from Nandi to Suva. Centered in the rainbow was the shadow of the airplane. God's covenant sign pinpointed the blessings available to those who go forth in His name.

Father LaBreque, our host in Suva, showed us around the city. He was Spirit-filled. He had hoped to attend the retreat himself and was delighted to take us.

Ralph's presentation ministered to the hearts of God's servants in Fiji. We joined with him in the prayer ministry. The room was filled with vigorous praise. The Holy Spirit distributed gifts of tongues and prophecy freely among those who sought an outpouring of His power in their lives.

Even "en route" to our mission, the Lord was already using us in His service. He taught us to expect the unexpected.

Chapter Fourteen

Tongatapu, Sacred South

"*Malo e lei lei,*" stately Polynesians greeted us.

"That's Tongan for welcome," Father Fitzsimmons explained. He met us at the airport. He was in charge of St. John's High School where Frank would teach.

Brown-skinned children gathered around, flashing friendly smiles and acting as porters with the suitcases carried effortlessly on their heads. Already I loved the peaceful, happy Tongans.

The palm trees swayed in the gentle breeze and the sun danced off of the deep green branches still wet from a recent rain. As the jeep sped through the palm forested interior toward the sea, filtered sunlight fell on thatched huts. We drove past the amazing coastal blowholes and where the fruit bats "hung around." We drove down the street in front of the King's palace. When the jeep reached the final mile along the clear, azure, ocean front, we got very, very quiet. It was gorgeous.

Colorful Tongan fishing boats and a few "round the world" sailing yachts were docked in the beautiful calm water.

"Father Fitzsimmons, were those policemen or soldiers who crossed pedestrians in the middle of town? I haven't seen one traffic light in Tonga. Do they have any?" Beau asked.

"They had to be policemen, so snappily dressed in those red, white and black uniforms, right?" I said.

"Traffic is not a not a problem here, there are buses, a few automobiles, and those motorcycle cabs over there with baskets on the back. But, to answer your question, no stoplights."

Frank pointed to the cyclists, and said, "The flat land is ideal for bicycles."

"There's St. Mary's Cathedral" Father Fitzsimmons pointed to a large coral rock cathedral. "The rocks were hand hewn by the first islander converts to Catholicism. And right over there is your house."

The little red and yellow frame house that was to be our new home overlooked the sea. It was situated on one corner of the cathedral compound.

Our "house" was a building left behind by an engineering firm which came to Tonga to construct the cruise ship wharf. The church had lent them the land, and afterward the little house became church property.

Captain Cook had called these the friendly isles. They lived up to the name. *Mau'fanga* was the Catholic settlement on the edge of the capital city of *Nukualofa*. Nukualofa means "abode of love" and *Tongatapu* means "sacred South." A tall, young Polynesian girl, wearing a lovely red hibiscus behind her ear, was standing on our porch. She was holding a basket of fruit in her hands.

She said in a melodic, slightly British accent, "Good Day, we're not finished cleaning out your house. The Sisters from St. Mary's College are sending over some clean sheets."

"Thank you, that's so kind of you. I'd like to use the bathroom and maybe then we can go over to the Cathedral and say a prayer. Where is the bathroom?" I asked.

"Follow me, I'll show you," she said and walked off the front porch, around the side of our neighbor's house (they were New Zealand Volunteers). She crossed in front of a storage

Go! You Are Sent   **138**

building and about a half block away from our front door, reached a small building which contained two cold water showers and two toilet stalls.

"These are flush toilets," she said proudly.

"So I do have an outhouse," I thought. "And she's right, thank God the toilets flush. Later, when I was really tired, I used to call my last trip to the bathroom at night my "penitential walk". I offered those night walks as a sacrifice of prayer for my loved ones.

"Hey, mate, you want to go walking to the pier?" two young boys called out to Beau from behind the palm tree in that same melodic accent.

Beau cocked his head to the side, glanced up at us for approval and ran off with his new found friends.

When we were finally able to enter the house, we found it to be very, very simple —four conservative rooms sparsely furnished. The largest bedroom had a double bed, but not a double bed mattress. Two small mattresses were placed side by side on a double frame. The mattresses were not of the same height, one was quite a bit higher than the other. A small washbowl, and a small cabinet were its only contents.

Beau's room had one small chest of drawers and a single cot. The cot was a cross between a bed and a hammock with a flimsy kapok mattress. Mosquito nets protected us at night from insect bites —or almost did! In the morning, it always seemed as though Beau caught more mosquitoes in his net than he kept out.

A small living room; small kitchen with a two burner gas stove, no oven; a sink for washing dishes; and a refrigerator that sometimes worked. There was a set of six chairs and a table.

We put our suitcases down in our new Tongan home, and went into the cathedral to pray. "Thank you, Lord, for the poverty and simplicity you have provided for us. Thank you, Lord, for the friendly people. Thank you, Lord, for safe travel, for peace and protection. You are truly a mighty God."

We got settled in the house, had dinner with the Marist priests that evening, and found that we had about four days before the beginning of school and teacher's orientation. We needed to get a "move on" in order to be settled and ready. Beau and I went to borrow an alarm clock from one of our neighbors.

"You won't need the clock to wake you up in the morning, you definitely won't sleep through the drums," she assured us.

"What drums?" Beau asked.

"Right in front of the rectory over there," she pointed, "the hollowed out log is a drum. They beat the drum every morning for five to ten minutes to wake up the villagers in time for daily mass."

"We don't want to miss Mass," I insisted, "Maybe we won't wake up."

"Oh, you'll wake up all right" she answered, "but if it makes you feel any better, I'll lend you the clock."

Early the next day, we were awakened to the thundering, pounding of the drums. Our first mission post was going to be intriguing.

Early in the morning it was cool enough for a light sweater. We walked toward the cathedral as the sun was rising and the light was breaking through the invigorating mist that rolled in from the ocean.

Happy smiles greeted us as the daily mass regulars noticed the new *Pa'alangi* family. "Pa'alangis" were the white people. The name came from the first missionaries and explorers who

Go! You Are Sent 140

came over the horizon on boats, as from the sky. It meant "they come from the sky."

Just before daily mass started, the congregation began to sing. They did sing like angels! We couldn't understand the words, but we could understand the worship, and Jesus came to us in the Eucharist. We understood more clearly than ever the meaning of the word "Catholic —universal." The drums, the barefoot Eucharist minister, the singing in harmonized parts of every mass response was so different from mass at home, and yet, it was the same. Being at mass was being at home, at home in my Father's house even in a strange land.

Tongans told us that they didn't have a word for privacy. They live a very community oriented life. Right after breakfast, we had several little children on our porch staring in our windows, as well as a few adults.

"Would you like to come in?" we asked invitingly.

"No, thank you, we're just looking", was the response.

Beau's new friends were a young boy named Isitolo, and his brother Soane. A young girl named Lesieli and a sixteen year old named Williami helped us get our bearings. They brought us to the market, introduced us to the corner grocer, and brought us our first coconuts —the green ones that are for drinking. We were amazed at the art of choosing and opening a just right coconut. Drinking the refreshing juice and then eating the tender meat of the young coconuts is a memorable experience.

Coconuts are the principal export of the country. Each Tongan male reaching the age of sixteen came into possession of eight acres of land. He was then to plant coconut trees. Under the coconut trees he could also farm root crops and fruit trees.

Generosity is one of the hallmarks of the Tongan culture. If we even slightly indicated we liked anything that they could bring us, like avocados, papayas, coconuts, and breadfruit, we would be overwhelmed with them.

At the same time, they expected generosity from you.

"You have three blouses and I don't have any; you should give me one," they could say with no qualms about it.

Most of their houses had very little furniture. They slept on woven mats, and ate on the mats, too. Instead of plates, they usually ate on banana leaves with their fingers. The clean-up afterward was so simple. I often wondered why I couldn't get into it. The Lord showed us how well they lived in community. If He wanted us to learn about simplicity, sharing and community, He had brought us to the right place.

Several crises cropped up for me in the first few days. I had brought mainly pants suits and jeans to wear. I had a couple of church dresses. Women in Tonga didn't wear pants. Not only that, the teachers at St. Mary's High School were not allowed to wear pants. Crisis number one, what should I wear?

Modesty was a very important part of the way of life. Even the men were not allowed to have their shoulders exposed, which meant men had to wear shirts, except when they were working on their farms. Modesty in dress and demeanor typified the culture. Over blouses of colorful tropical prints matched the women's graceful skirts that skimmed the ground. The men wore a sort of wrap-around knee length "skirt" or *Tupenu*, with a matching tee shirt. Most wore simple sandals or went barefoot.

The adults wore woven mats, *Taovala*, of varying widths around their waists. We later learned that the width of the mat, as well as its "newness" or "oldness" had cultural significance.

It's wasn't long before I realized that Jesus brought me half-way around the world to train me in the importance of modesty.

He spoke to my heart very clearly. "If a man commits adultery in his heart by looking lustfully at a woman, surely the woman commits adultery by dressing so as to provoke temptation and desire."

Once or twice a month, cruise ships arrived from New Zealand, Australia, or Europe. Tourists disembarked in their summer wear. The contrast between them and the peaceful, modest Tongans was jolting. To solve my "what to wear" crisis, Lesieli brought me to a dressmaker and helped me pick out material. I had some long, flowing dresses made. In no time at all, I felt comfortable and feminine. Frank liked my new dresses a lot. Crisis number one solved.

Before I left for mission, I felt that I was prepared to face any hardship or difficulty because I loved Jesus, and nothing would be too hard to endure for Him. I could picture myself hacking my way through a jungle with a machete, washing and bathing in a stream, and cooking over an open fire. Thank God that he knows every hair on my head, and that he didn't send me first to that jungle situation. I actually cried the first time I took a cold shower. The first time I used a washboard, I prayed and washed, prayed and washed. I was surprised to find myself so inept at a task the gentle Tongan women made look so easy. The Lord had prepared a place for us. He hand-picked the trials and difficulties. He also opened the floodgates of heaven and blessings just kept flowing into my life while he trained me as His missionary.

There was only one elementary school that taught its curriculum in English. It was called Tonga Side School and most of the missionaries' children attended that school. Beau was accepted into the sixth grade. He had to bring his lunch and take a bus to school each day. We didn't worry a bit about him, because the island was so safe. Most people could not recall any violent crime that had taken place there.

Because he was a new kid, and also because he wore a wooden cross, he received a good bit of persecution. He fought the spiritual battle; and he finally won the esteem of his classmates as he kept "turning the other cheek" when pushed or shoved. A Protestant missionary told us that his son at Tonga Side School was deeply affected by Beau's witness.

Our house was always full of children that wanted to play with Beau or just hang around. Most evenings we shared our supper with eight or ten kids. We prayed and sang before every meal. The children frequently joined us for our family prayer time. Without a doubt, the Lord frequently multiplied our food. Sometimes, when it looked like we might have an extra serving, I expected someone else to show up. They usually did.

Soon, the children were bringing their sick relatives to our house for prayers and healing, and God answered those prayers. The spiritual lives of our Tongan friends and neighbors began to change before our very eyes. The gospel is good news and we were its humble heralds.

Neither Frank nor I were professional teachers. Getting into the mode of teaching English, lesson planning, giving tests and grading papers was all new to us. I, at least, got to teach religion to a group of teenage girls. It was exciting to watch these young women open their lives to the Lord Jesus and His Holy Spirit. Frank longed for more opportunities to share the word in outright evangelistic ministry.

He had plenty chances to evangelize "one-on-one". So few of the Catholics there had even heard of the renewal in the Holy Spirit within the church. Like most Christian third world cultures, their faith in God the father was strong. We longed to share with them how we came to have a close personal relationship with the Lord.

Our evangelistic outreach in Tonga mainly manifested itself in the testimony of our lives and relationships.

One day a very friendly lady about my age knocked on our front door. She held out a banana bread she had baked for us. I loved the New Zealand accent. I knew instinctively that we would be friends.

"Hi. I'm Gillian Laurenson, and these are Ruth and Michael. We live near the school and heard that you had arrived. Welcome to Tonga."

"Thanks. It's so gorgeous here. It's nice to meet you. Please come in. I'm Genie Summers, that's my son, Beau, out there at the sea wall. Frank will be back in a few minutes."

"We've been here a year now, so if you need to know anything, or need some help getting settled, let me know," she offered.

"The Tongans have been so helpful. Although, I must admit learning the language looks like a challenge to me. Beau is already picking up words, I guess children learn quickly," I said.

We chatted. She left and invited Frank, Beau and me to drop in and visit her family any time.

Ewen was Catholic and Gillian, Presbyterian, but as a family they worshipped at the Catholic Church. All masses were in Tongan, except for one English Mass every month. Protestant churches also held worship services in the native language.

The King made his small private chapel situated on the palace grounds available to English speaking Christians. The King was a Methodist and he preferred to worship in the main Methodist church. Because the Island was small, it was simple for the English Speaking Christians of every denomination to come to know one another. We met every Sunday evening. For Frank, Beau and me, it meant about a mile walk under the stars along the seashore. That was one of the most blessed ecumenical activities I've ever participated in.

Pastors, including Catholic priests, and lay people would take turns presenting a program of Bible sharing and prayer each Sunday. Frank and I went to Mass every morning, weekdays and Sundays. On Sunday evenings, we enjoyed the fellowship at the King's Chapel. Not only were we of various denominations, we were from many different nations, including English speaking Tongans. It was a joy to "sing praises to God among the nations."

The Laurensons and the Summers presented the service one night and we chose to talk on the topic of Christian joy. (After almost twenty years now of relating to this remarkable family, I still think of Christian joy when I think of them. Their time in Tonga, like ours, was a beginning of a life lived in service to Jesus.)

Ewen and Gillian opened their home several afternoons a week for a first aid clinic. Tropical sores, especially, plagued the children. The Laurensons knew that good hygiene and clean dressings were essential in combating the sores. Following their example, we, too, always kept first aid supplies, cleaned and dressed wounds as a service to the children.

Singing and praising God were an essential part of our prayer life. We missed the "Abba" prayer community, so we began a small meeting in one of the halls on the far side of the compound. Each week was a surprise. Jesus and the Holy Spirit were there, but we were never quite sure who else would show up.

Chapter Fifteen

Dengue, Doubts, Decisions

Soane, Beau's Tongan companion, came running into our house one night. He looked worried. I wondered if it was that a storm was brewing in the Pacific Ocean just a few yards away. Scarier than that was the news Soane brought.

"The peace corps worker, the peace corps worker that lives in the Fale (hut) by the school is blind. The Dengue fever has made him blind. It's pretty bad, you know."

"Who told you this, Soane?" Frank asked.

"I saw him myself, it's true," Soane affirmed his earlier report.

A Dengue fever epidemic spread over the Island of Tongatapu when we were there in 1975. Sixteen people died, mostly small babies or old people. And a young Peace Corps worker had to return to the U. S. because of temporary blindness, an after-effect of Dengue.

The Summers family didn't escape the epidemic. Both Frank and I succumbed at the same time. Raging fever accompanied by severe headaches, bone pain, weakness, depression, and finally, an unbearable itching of the hands and feet symptomized this disease. Thank God, Beau had a very mild case.

There is never a trial, that doesn't bring with it blessings. Sister Mary Joseph was one of those blessings. "Yoo hoo, can I come in?" a deep, happy voice called out at our door.

"Is there someone here who has Dengue fever? I heard you might need some help," she said as she walked in and made her way straight to our bedroom where Frank and I were both in bed, burning up with fever.

"Hello, Sister," I said. "Did Beau go for you?"

"No, not Beau. Lesieli told me all about it. I'm Sister Mary Joseph Beck. I'm from Australia and I've come to Tonga to take over the dispensary. Sister Mercedes is just getting too old."

"I had been helping Sister Mercedes a little bit until I got sick. We're glad to have you here, Sister Mary Joseph. What do you think about this epidemic?" Frank asked.

I think you two better get well, so you can help out some more. I've brought you some medications that won't cure you, but it'll make you more comfortable and maybe ward off secondary infections."

Beau walked in. "Are you the Sister that rides that Honda motor bike? I love it. Where did you live before you came to Tonga?" He questioned her.

"I've lived in the Solomon Islands most of my religious life, as a mission nurse. And in my dispensary, by sheer necessity, I was sometimes a general practitioner, gynecologist, midwife, surgeon, and pathologist," Sister explained.

Her daily visits to our home were a ray of sunshine during our weeks of Dengue fever. When Dengue fever discouraged us in our vocation as missionaries, the Lord won the victory by sending us a living model of a joyful, persevering saint. Sister Mary Joseph treasured the call to mission as the pearl of great price. When we recovered from the fever, Frank volunteered regularly to help her in the dispensary.

Father Martin in Franklin, Louisiana had his parish send a thousand dollars worth of medical supplies to Sister Mary

Joseph's dispensary. Their lenten collections were dedicated that year to help our mission. We learned that a benefit of mission life was connecting the church in Louisiana with God's work in Tonga. Jesus said that "whatsoever you do to the least of my brothers, that you do unto me." The parishioners in Franklin met the medical needs of Jesus' brothers and sisters in Tonga.

Other hassles and difficulties of the new life we had chosen surfaced in this first mission. These hassles have not gone away, and we are still certain that the only way to handle them is with patience and prayer. Finances —a missionary's struggle over finances is part and parcel of the vocation. We walk in faith, but we need support. The Lord has *never* failed to supply our needs according to His riches in glory.

Many times, the Summers family has cried out to Him, "Lord, we are facing financial disaster!"

More often than not, the rescue came only at the eleventh hour.

Frank had a source of personal income, royalty income, that varied greatly over the years. Banking over great distances can be frustrating. Handling the money needed to sustain a family serving the Lord in a foreign land is always a challenge. Deposit slips can be delayed in the mail. Checks can be held over for two or three months. Any number of things that can go wrong in accounting and often do. We have needed to keep on trusting in Jesus. More than once, we were caught without funds.

In Tonga, Frank and I were paid fifty dollars a month each, and we tried to live on that. Our friends, the Tongans, brought us gifts of food that helped to stretch the budget. We got paid twice a month.

One Friday, our pay wasn't due until Monday. We didn't have anything at all in the pantry. We were waiting for funds

Dengue, Doubts, Decisions

from home that hadn't arrived. I hated to ask the sisters to lend us the money. I went to of St. Mary's High School Chapel, where I daily had my personal prayer time.

"Lord Jesus, you tell us not to worry about what we are to eat and what we are to drink; I know that worry is useless, but please help me to trust." I bowed my head and felt the anointing of the Holy Spirit.

As I finished teaching for the day, I was trusting a little and wondering a lot, "What in the world will we have for supper?"

The sister in charge of the paychecks stopped me. She said, "Genie, I hope you don't mind if we pay you today instead of Monday. I never made it to the bank today, and I'm afraid to keep too much money in the school office over the weekend."

"Thank you, Sister," I said shaking her hand vigorously.

I skipped home.

"Mom, I thought we weren't going to have anything to eat, tonight," Beau asked. He had come in wet from a swim. "Did we get some money or something?"

"God did provide, Beau, as he always does. We prayed and I got paid early."

That night we ate mackerel salad sandwiches. We substituted canned mackerel for tuna in our salad. It was cheaper. Isitolo brought us papaya. We feasted.

Frank read us the day's mail after supper. "This letter's from Judge Putnam. I'm happy he took time to write, he's so busy."

The judge's letter teased Frank about living in paradise, "You can't fool me. I'm sure you spend most of the day under blue skies and palm trees, watching the ocean and reeling gulls. No wonder you left us here in the rat race."

The teasing pointed to a truth that is very hard for busy Americans to learn. Here in Tonga, we were learning. The rat race is not God's plan for us, His people. Time is a gift. God wanted our family to live an abundant, full life focusing on the things He thinks are important.

Frank and I found, at first, that we had a built in resistance to slowing down to the pace of life on a small tropical island. After a while, we settled into a wonderful routine. School let out at two in the afternoon. My days were pretty full with teaching, housekeeping, marketing, washing and cooking. We waited for Beau to come home from school and we would swim in the ocean.

The Marist priest's community had a wonderful library with books on church history, papal documents, *L'Osservatore Romano*, Bible Commentaries, and teachings by leading theologians. Frank was able to take advantage of his free time to read, pray and study. Once or twice a week we had dinner with our Christian friends, in our home or theirs. Up to ten children, and occasional adults, just "happened" by and joined with us in daily family prayer. But, most of all, we really enjoyed our family time. Living in a foreign culture drew our family close together.

It wasn't all roses. We did things that irritated our neighbors. The scores of children who were always at our house played noisily in the yard. They used the toilet we had in common with our neighbors and stopped it up with too much paper. "Tim" and "Ann" (names changed) felt that our nightly singing and prayer intruded on their peace and quiet. They blamed their discontent on our being "Christians".

Tim was not convinced that Jesus was the only way. One day, he and Frank were in a discussion of religion, and Tim kept asking Frank why follow Jesus and not Zoroaster, or Buddha, or Mohammed.

Finally, Frank said, "Tim, we can sit here arguing about whether or not it's raining outside. I'll probably never convince you that it is, but if you go outside and get wet, you'll be convinced. If you want to know if Jesus is the Son of God, and you sincerely bow before Him and ask Him to reveal Himself to you, He will. You will be convinced. 'He who seeks, finds!' Kneel down before Jesus tonight in humble prayer and you'll know for sure that He is Lord!"

I don't know if Tim ever prayed that prayer, but one day I caught him humming the tune of *"Oh, Oh, Oh, How Good is the Lord"* as he worked in his garden.

Beau couldn't possibly have had a better place to be ten years old. He, too, did a lot of reading, especially in the Bible. He had swarms of friends. Some became like brothers to him. They fished and explored the island. Beau often went out with Soane and Isitolo to their farm under the coconut trees. They played on the wharf and made friends with all the sailors who sailed around the world.

One of his most vivid memories is watching his friend, Isitolo, slash his machete at a fish swimming by in the shallow water, "spear it", and bring the fish home for supper. Beau finally learned to climb a coconut tree, rather slowly, but he climbed them nonetheless —a real accomplishment for a Pa'alangi.

The school Beau attended offered guitar lessons, so we ordered a guitar for Beau. It arrived too late for the Beau's lessons, but when it did come in, Frank decided he would learn to play. We always sang in our prayer time, we had even taught Williami our songs, but they never sounded exactly the way we sang them at home. Frank rode his bike down to the only bookstore on the island and found a book that was entitled, "Play the Guitar in Twenty Minutes."

Go! You Are Sent 152

As he sat down to learn, he gathered Beau and me in prayer. He said, "Lord if you will give me the gift of playing the guitar, I promise I will only use it to sing songs for your glory."

It was exciting to see Frank learn so fast. The Lord bestowed on him a gift that would become very useful in our missionary life.

One of the young girls in my religion class was named Sanita. She was very thin, sickly, and had missed a lot of school. She spent a lot of time with us after school, too. Sanita was crying one day as I entered the classroom. I asked her why she was so sad.

She sniffled, "Today is my last day of school. My doctor has told me that I need to stay in my house from now on." I didn't know exactly what her diagnosis was. "I've had an enlarged heart since my birth, and I can hardly catch my breath sometimes. Now the doctor says if I don't stay home and rest, I might die. I don't want to quit school, Mrs. Summers, can Jesus heal me?"

We had talked a lot about Jesus and that his miracles didn't stop happening two thousand years ago.

I told her, "Sanita, Jesus can heal you. Why don't you come to our house after school and we will pray for you. We will ask Him for the miracle you need."

For several months we had been praying for Sanita. Her absence from school had worried me, and we even sent prayer requests to people at home to pray for her; but I hadn't known about the enlarged heart. We prayed over her with the laying on of hands. It was an anointed prayer time. Sanita asked us to visit her at home. She would be seeing her doctor again in two or three days.

Dengue, Doubts, Decisions

What a surprise it was to see her on the basketball court, dribbling the ball at school at the end of that same week. When she spotted me, she waved a big hello.

I called to her, "Sanita, come here. Tell me what has happened."

She sighed happily, "I'm healed, completely healed. My doctor says he's never seen anything like it. He's been monitoring my heart since I was born. 'It can only be a miracle!' he said. 'God must have some special plan for your life!'"

"Sanita, how beautiful. Thank you, Jesus, for healing Sanita," I said, giving her a big hug.

"Maybe I can become a nun, like I told you I wanted to," she exclaimed excitedly. I shook my head in amazement as she ran back onto the court, joining the game again.

Despite all the good things that were going on in our lives, Frank's desire to be in a full-time evangelistic ministry grew stronger and stronger. He talked to the priests and sisters at the schools. He offered to serve in the parish. Everyone told us they would try to help us find the opportunity to do more in evangelism, but nothing turned up. Finally, we went to talk to Bishop Finau, with whom we had a very good relationship. We offered to serve the diocese in evangelism in any way he could use us.

For awhile, the Bishop seriously considered sending us to an island which had no priest to live among the people. It was an active volcano. A priest only visited there every six months, staying a few weeks to celebrate marriages, baptisms and first communions. Supply ships rarely went there and the island was only accessible by small fishing boats. That island is referred to as "Tin Can Island" because supplies have to be sealed in drums and floated to the shore from larger vessels. It would be

Go! You Are Sent 154

a risky place for a family. Bishop Finau asked us to go home and think about it for a week.

We prayed, talked, and thought about it. There was so much involved in accepting this kind of assignment. Beau was now eleven and full of zeal for the Lord. It sounded exciting to him and he wanted to go. But if we ended up staying several years, would he still be happy there?

For us, there were other important considerations. Before we had come into mission, we had been ill advised about the church's stand on artificial birth control.

When we first arrived in Tonga, we were happy with our small family and were still practicing artificial contraception. The little mission house we moved into had only two books left behind from the former tenant. One of those books was Pope Paul VI's encyclical on Human Life —*Humanae Vitae*. Frank read the book from cover to cover, seeing and understanding the language as a lawyer would.

He called me into our bedroom one day. "Babe," he held my hand and his eyes looked troubled, "this document is very clear. We've been wrong. The Catholic Church in no way condones artificial birth control. There are no loopholes."

"I should have seen this sooner. Probably that's why we had so much trouble bringing a year's supply of pills. What should we do? I do not want to be locked into anything that God doesn't want for me, but in a way I'm afraid," I said with my voice breaking.

"I've been to talk to Father Collin and he told me that there is a sister here who teaches natural family planning. He thinks she would be happy to teach us the method. We need to meet with her as soon as possible."

I was floored. We held hands and cried together. What did it mean for us? If we opened our lives to more children, could we continue in the work of missionaries? In brokenness and humble obedience we said, "Yes, Lord."

The transition was easier than we thought it would be. All we had to do was radically repent, keep a chart, and move on to greater faithfulness.

Now that the Tin Can Island thing was being presented to us, we realized that it was possible that I would get pregnant and give birth in a situation with little or no medical help available. Could we tell the Bishop "yes" in light of all that? When we went to his office the next week, we had decided to accept the offer if he made it.

Much to our disappointment, the Bishop had changed his mind. He felt he couldn't bear the responsibility for an American family in a situation he considered truly dangerous.

Now we were in a dilemma. We had declared our need to find a full-time evangelistic ministry in Tonga. We loved the place and its people. Our only recourse was to have a family retreat. We needed to hear the Lord. Again, we committed our future to serve wherever He called us. Begging Him for a work in which we would be better engaged in evangelism, we trusted Him to answer us.

Jesus said, "I must proclaim the Good News of the Kingdom of God." (Luke 4:43)

St. Paul wrote to the Corinthians "Not that I boast of preaching the gospel, since it is a duty that has been laid on me; I should be punished if I did not preach it!" (9:16).

The Catholic bishops have said, "We wish to confirm once more that the task of evangelizing all people constitutes the essential mission of the church."

In our family retreat, the Lord clearly showed us to move on, to go. Scripture, visions, and leadings from the Lord were strong and consistent. Frank received a vision that showed us leaving Tonga on a boat heading into the rising sun. Cruise ships came to the island, but we knew of none that went East. Questioning the one travel agent in town confirmed this.

"How Lord?" The question was bearing down on Frank as he rode his bike back from the travel agent's office. Suddenly, he noticed a rather battered cargo tug boat at the wharf.

"This can hardly be it. This tug has an unsettling list to the port side," he thought.

The crew of the "Lady Lata" was busy unloading crates.

"Where does this boat go?" Frank asked.

"Tomorrow afternoon we sail for American Samoa."

Frank knew that Samoa was East of Tonga. "Do you take passengers? How much does it cost?"

"We take passengers that sleep on the covered deck. The cost is $24 dollars per person, and you must provide your own food. You can buy the tickets at our office in town."

"Can we be ready by tomorrow afternoon? That's the big question." Frank asked me after he told me all about the "Lady Lata."

I was more than a little leery, and it didn't quite measure up to my thoughts of sailing out on a cruise ship, but I heard the Lord Jesus say in my heart, "This is my plan."

"We've already told the schools and most of our friends that we would be leaving soon. Soane's been crying for two weeks. I'll be happy not to prolong the good-byes any longer. It's too painful."

"Yeah, Mom, but can we pack that fast?" Beau asked. He had mixed feelings. Yet, he trusted our guidance.

"Packing won't be a problem, we have so few things!" I explained to them, "I love to be on the sea. I'm getting kind of excited about it."

At the ticket office, Frank learned that he couldn't purchase the tickets without an "exit" visa. The exit visa required twenty-two signatures from government agencies attesting to the fact that you didn't owe any money anywhere in the Kingdom. Only then were you free to leave Tonga.

Frank prayed, "Father, we believe this to be your plan. I don't even know where most of these offices are. What if some are not open? It'll take a miracle to get all these signatures in one afternoon. Send your angels before me, please Lord."

The miracle was granted, and we boarded ship, having said a final prayer in the coral rock cathedral. Father Collin and the sisters gave us a ride to the wharf. Our generous friends loaded us down with gifts of food for the journey. There were more than thirty people on the wharf to see us off. Most were in tears as the crew threw off the ropes and hoisted the anchor. Soane, who had practically lived with us, was sobbing hysterically.

It was then we learned the lesson that is hardest of all about Mission life —saying good-bye.

We loved them. They were our real friends. Because we had come, they knew Jesus better.

We had struggled with doubts, suffered from Dengue, and made decisions that would forever change our lives. The love of Jesus and the lasting friendships we formed in Tonga filled my heart and allowed me to be propelled forward from there to an uncertain future. The Lady Lata pulled away from the wharf. Soon, our little yellow and red frame house near the ocean faded away. A significant part of my heart remained peacefully under the palm trees of our first mission post, but a significant part of my mission character had been formed there.

This is how all will know you are my disciples; your love for one another.   (John 13:35)

Chapter Sixteen

The Molokau

Our ocean-going tugboat rocked and lurched on the stormy sea. The gentle Tongans aboard never complained or showed fear. Several were seasick. Passengers slept on the open deck. Bench seats wrapped around the stern, and a metal roof kept off the sun and rain. The faulty design of the boat trapped exhaust fumes under the roof, much to the discomfort of the passengers. During rain or storms, canvas flaps were lowered and the fumes nauseated and sickened us.

It was our first night out. We had been told it would be a five day voyage from Tonga to Samoa, with one night in Vava'u, and one day on a small out-island. Our mats were rolled out, and we were trying to get comfortable on deck as best we could. I fought my way to the bathroom, only to discover that it was flooded with six inches of water, which swished around and made its own little sea.

Pieces of toilet paper floated there. Curtains meant to provide privacy for the stalls dragged through the water and moved back and forth with the waves.

This was a different style of traveling, not like the jet planes that had taken us to Tonga. Beau, Frank and I snuggled under our blanket the first night out. We realized that we were one with the people we served. We traveled as they traveled.

The guitar tied to the luggage rack swung wildly above our heads as the storm tossed us about. A big wave hit and we tumbled together. Righting ourselves, we saw one of our mission crosses fall overboard.

"There goes my mission cross," Frank said.

"I hope that's not a sign that we're next," I said.

"All we can do is trust the Lord, Babe."

So we entrusted ourselves to Jesus and finally fell asleep.

The rising sun awakened us. The sea was calm again.

"Gosh, this is a beautiful morning," I leaned over the rail to peer into the immensely deep, blue sea.

"At least the wind is blowing the fumes away from us today, Thank God," Frank said, noticing the difference not breathing the fumes made. "Let's pray, I don't think the guitar will bother anyone."

Most of the Polynesian passengers joined us, and we shared our faith with them.

Later that morning, everyone rushed to our side of the deck. Whales playfully surfaced nearby. An awareness of our holy adventure returned to us. The Lord Jesus entertained us with a show from his mighty creatures from the deep.

Travel guides say Vava'u's harbor is the most beautiful in the world. The Summers family thought it was pretty spectacular after our trip up from Tonagatapu. However, Tonga's showpiece is one of those ends of God's earth rarely seen or appreciated by outsiders. The sailing schedule of the Lady Lata allowed for one night there. We planned to stay with relatives of our friend, Lesieli. She accompanied us as far as Vava'u. Lesieli's elderly aunt and uncle welcomed us warmly. They had one of the few two story houses on the island. It was very simple.

It was good to be on shore again. After a fine meal and a good night's sleep, we awakened the next morning ready to be on our way to American Samoa. We packed and were about to walk down to the wharf with our luggage. Evidently, the Tongans on Vava'u were more accustomed to the Lady Lata's irregularities in sailing than we were, and insisted on sending Lesieli ahead to see if the boat was indeed going to depart at the proper time.

To our surprise, she came back with very disconcerting news. The Lady Lata was having engine trouble and would return to Tongatapu for repairs. What we thought would be one night stretched to a ten day stay.

Our hosts allowed us to share in the expenses and truly seemed to enjoy our visit.

The second day, Frank came back to the home where we were staying and said, "I had a chance to share our testimony with the parish priest. He is trying to arrange for us to give a talk to families in the parish."

"Well, we begged the Lord to use us in evangelism. He's already doing it. That's wonderful, Frank."

"It seems it's pretty easy to spread the word around here. He'll let us know something definite soon," Frank continued.

"I think we'll have fun here," Beau said. "Maybe this is God's delay."

Our days were spent exploring the lovely island, relaxing, and imbibing God's love. Eight days later, the Lady Lata came back and was scheduled to leave for Samoa the next morning.

We ventured out for one last swim at a nearby beach, and happened on a family we knew. They invited us to share in their feast. The food was good, but as we walked the road back, Beau began to complain of a terrible headache.

"Mom, I don't think the octopus was well done. I feel really bad, kinda weird, and I'm itchy all over."

The Molokau

"Your whole body is covered with red bumps. You're having an allergic reaction," I said, and gave him aspirin for his headache.

"Frank, I don't like the looks of this and I don't have any Benadryl left after the Dengue fever. I don't know what we should do." I had cornered him.

"I'm not too worried, we'll watch it and as long as it doesn't get any worse, we don't have anything to worry about. Let's pray over him for healing," Frank said as he walked over to the cot Beau was laying on.

Supper time found Beau feeling a little better. He ate a few keke, a Tongan version of beignets. Then he reached for a towel to dry his hands.

"Ow, oh, ouch! ow!" Beau suddenly recoiled and screamed in pain.

"What is it, Son?" I asked in a panic.

Beau screamed and jumped up and down.

"Molokau! Molokau!" Lesieli shouted as she shook a horrible, black, poisonous, three inch centipede out of the napkin Beau had grabbed.

The relatives from downstairs had come up at the sound of the commotion and were conversing rapidly in Tongan. I kept hearing the word "molokau" and saw a lot of head shaking.

Beau had been stung by a *molokau*. Deaths were sometimes attributed to their bites. Due to the allergic reaction that his body was already fighting, Beau got sick, really sick, fast! In an hour, his fever was raging.

Our lodgings had no electricity. By the light of an oil lamp, Frank and I were at his head and his feet mopping him with cool water to lower his fever. He had severe vomiting and diarrhea. There was no bathroom, only an outhouse. We lifted him precariously onto a chamber pot. Soon he was delirious, tossing and turning violently. I was giving him aspirin every three hours but to no avail. The fever didn't respond at all.

I called Frank out of the room where Beau lay suffering. I put my hands on his arms and looked him straight in the eyes. "We'd better get him to the doctor, it's serious!"

We asked our hosts where the doctor lived, or if there was a hospital.

"There are no doctors living on the island. Paramedics and medical students man a small hospital," Lesieli's uncle said.

"It's too far away to walk there and the motorcycle cabs don't run this late at night. How will you take him?" Lesieli asked.

"The priest has a car," the uncle answered.

Frank went to ask the priest to drive us there. When we got to the hospital, there were electric lights. We gasped in shock to see how terrible Beau looked in the light! He was absolutely limp, and was wine-colored over most of his body. There were bluish white splotches around his mouth. The paramedics looked frightened as they examined him. They said there was little they could do. We should continue with the aspirin. They gave us some antihistamine tablets that we hoped and prayed he would keep down.

No beds were available, so we took him back to the house. He vomited up the medicine. Still the fever raged. Needless to say, we had been praying over Beau since the first moment he complained of a headache. We anointed him with oil again. I panicked. What was God doing!?

In the vision Frank had received at the farm before we left, Frank had seen the Lord's hand holding a little blond boy looking limp and dead. At that time, we had been made to understand that He was asking us if we would go, accept his call to be missionaries, even if it meant losing Beau!

The Molokau

In the anointing of the moment we had said, "Yes, Lord," and then the child came back to life. Knowing that Beau was now at death's door, we remembered that "Yes, Lord."

We were very quiet, both of us. The church clock struck midnight. Nothing had changed. Beau was still tossing and mumbling deliriously.

I began to pray, "Lord, I surrender my beautiful son, Beau, to you. Thank you for every minute of our eleven years with him." Tears streamed down my face and quiet sobs broke the silence.

"Thank you, Lord, for each moment he's been mine. Thank you for his first laugh in the bathtub when the toy ducks bounced up and down. Thanks for the time we spent reading Shakespeare together when he was only four years old. Thank you for the strolls through Trafalgar Square and the climb up to the Acropolis. Thanks for the wisdom he's shared in our prayer times. Oh, Jesus, Oh, dear Lord, I'll miss him so much. Thank you that he really did learn to climb a coconut tree. Help me, Lord, I'll miss him so much. He's Yours. I know that. Take him if it's time. Please, give me peace."

I could feel that same surrender in Frank. The Lord's peace settled on me like a blanket. The room seemed to fill with a warm light. Beau relaxed and fell into a peaceful sleep. His fever dropped drastically. The vomiting ceased. I fell asleep, exhausted, at the foot of the bed.

The morning light dawned on a very weak little boy. He was still wine-colored, but a little bit hungry, which was a good sign.

A heavy decision faced us. The Lady Lata sailed for Samoa in the late morning. It's next trip to Vava'u was a month later. Small private planes could fly us back to the main island of Tongatapu, but we didn't have the money.

Go! You Are Sent 164

Everyone was terrified for us to get on the boat, including Beau and I. It wasn't an easy situation.

We entered into prayer. Frank was decisive.

"The Lord says to go on to Samoa."

We carried Beau aboard.

Beau looked so bad that the officials let us on first, and we laid him down. I was trying to trust, but our friends were on the dock crying. It was possible that Beau would die at sea.

As the ship sailed out the harbor, I could feel the Lord's peace descend on us again. The moment we hit the open sea, Beau jumped up, completely healed!! He wandered around the ship, made friends with the captain, and climbed on the crates of watermelons. He was the only passenger aboard that didn't get seasick on this last leg of the voyage. We praised Jesus for His faithfulness.

Cruising into Pago Pago, we were pleasantly surprised —it was a beautiful city! The harbor is very large and scenic. We were super-ready to leave the Lady Lata and our adventures of the last two weeks behind. How would we serve the Lord in this Polynesian "paradise"? We wondered how "American" American Samoa would be.

Beau said, "Maybe they'll have a Kentucky Fried Chicken place."

Frank laughed, "I hope not, I hope it's like Tonga."

American immigration officials were waiting for the passengers as we docked. And we were surprised to learn that they expected us to have tourist visas before we disembarked, even though we were American citizens. Tears welled up in my eyes and the Lord must have nudged them to have mercy on us.

"If you don't have visas, then you must have hotel reservations to show that you are tourists," they told us.

The Molokau

"Where are the hotels? Can I go ashore to find a room?" Frank asked, almost pleading.

"Yes, you may go," an official said. "But your wife and son have to stay here in the compound. I hope you have some luck. Someone just told me that the hotels are full. There are three of them, but only one is within walking distance."

We huddled together to say a quick prayer. Jesus had to come through for us again —He had brought us this far. We couldn't even bear to think of having to take the return voyage on the Lady Lata. Beau and I waited in the small compound behind a hurricane fence, praying. It was like being without a country. And it seemed like forever until Frank returned.

Chapter Seventeen

Pago Pago

Frank was smiling as he walked down the hill toward the compound. He went straight into the immigration official's office. But he called out over the fence. "Good news. I got the last hotel room on the island."

"Praise God," Beau and I said in unison. We relaxed and readied our baggage. An hour and a half in any kind of confinement against your wishes drags by. We rejoiced at being free to explore Pago Pago.

"Come on in here to sign these papers," Frank motioned to us. "The officials granted us short-term tourist visas."

"Maybe they gave us such a hard time because we don't look like ordinary Americans. After all, how many tourists arrive with most of their belongings wrapped in a Tongan mat?" I said, as we left the dock area.

"Yeah, and my guitar is in a British mail rucksack," Frank laughed.

Tired and feeling isolated from anything familiar, we sat and rested for a few minutes on a bench looking out at the beautiful harbor. In Tonga, we had been received by the Marists. Here, we knew not a single soul.

We walked up the hill to the hotel. Our room was small and the windows opened over an alley, not a very pretty view.

"This is God's providence. Thank you, God, for this room," and I meant it.

"The air conditioner works," Beau said standing directly in front of it, absorbing cold air.

"I don't know about y'all, but I hope the hot showers work," Frank said grabbing some clean clothes.

We would have to live off a few traveler's checks until we could open a bank account and arrange to have money transferred from the States. Finding a rent house quickly would be a priority because we couldn't afford to stay in the hotel. We'd have to trust the Lord for an extension on our visas.

There was a whole lot we could have worried about, but the grace of mission was upholding us, and we were trusting in the Lord's plan.

We bathed, took a nap, and then set out to explore our new surroundings.

"Look over there, I think that's the Catholic Church, maybe we can talk to the priest and find out what ministry Jesus has for us here." I said pointing in the direction of the center of town.

"Let's head in that direction," Frank said.

It was at about 5:45 in the evening. We heard bells ringing all over the island. Then everything got quiet. Traffic stopped. Children quit playing and went indoors. Indoors is not really the best way to describe it, because the native Samoan houses don't have walls.

We continued walking along, wondering what could be going on. Before we knew it, a man stepped out of his house and rather gruffly asked us to sit down on his doorstep.

"Can you please tell us what's happening?" Frank asked.

He replied, "In Samoa, we have a law that requires every person to stop everything for fifteen minutes in the morning and fifteen minutes in the afternoon to pray. If you don't want to pray, you must at least sit here and respect our prayers."

"Thank you, sir. Our family loves to pray. We're missionaries," I told him.

"Wow! That's really neat!" Beau exclaimed.

"We just didn't know. Thanks for telling us," Frank said, shaking the man's hand.

We sat down and bowed our heads, marveling at a country that requires daily prayer. Surely there was a place for us here. We remembered the Sabbath law that Tongans observed. Only worship and family gatherings were allowed on Sunday in Tonga —no recreation, no radio, no fishing, no selling, no work of any kind, except for simple meals almost totally prepared on Saturday night. Tongans kept Holy the Lord's Day. The King rode around the island surveying the good conduct of his constituents. And now, here we were in Samoa with their daily prayer law. Our American money says, "In God we trust," but we Americans had forbidden prayer in public schools. What a stark contrast!

Inquiring about rent houses was discouraging. According to people we met in the hotel, in the post office, and at the local grocery store, rent houses were hard to find. When you did find one, they were very expensive. Frank bought a newspaper. A few unfurnished apartments were listed, and there was one ad for a house. The house claimed to be "fully furnished". It was not in Pago Pago proper, but in a little settlement about a fifteen minute bus ride away.

The village chief of Laulii had the house for rent. He was very nice. He wore the traditional Samoan wrap-around called the "lava-lava". The house was a two bedroom wood frame house with walls, built to be hurricane-proof.

"Fully furnished" meant four wooden chairs (the kind we would use for lawn chairs in the South), a long slatted wooden bench, which we used as Beau's bed. The second bedroom had nothing at all inside. Polynesians were perfectly comfortable sleeping on their woven mats. That's what Frank and I used.

A picnic table with benches furnished the small dining room, and there was a sink and cabinets in the kitchen. That was it.

Location was the "plus" of the house. We could walk to the village Catholic church, and we could see the ocean from our front windows. The village houses were close together. There were kids for Beau to play with. We did have a flush toilet indoors and a shower with fairly good water pressure. If we bathed in the middle of the day, the water was nice and hot because the pipes were above ground and heated by the sun. There was no fridge. We purchased a one burner kerosene stove.

The priest in charge of the small village church was another Father Fitzsimmons, the brother of our friend in Tonga. He only came on Sunday. The parish was pastored by a Samoan catechist who lived on the church grounds with his wife and family.

As we realized how the catechist set-up worked, we were more puzzled about what God had for us to do there. We couldn't speak Samoan, and even though the majority spoke English, the services and catechism were conducted in the native tongue. Father Fitz took us under his wing, and asked Frank to accompany him on his visits to villages over the mountains.

The scriptures say, "They that wait upon the Lord will renew their strength." The first few weeks in the village of Laulii were more important than we could have suspected as we began to live them. We drenched our lives in prayer. The Lord led us into deeper repentance. More than ever before, we walked in the light with one another, seeking reconciliation and openness.

Go! You Are Sent 170

Every day as I cooked and washed by hand, I was surrounded by many little Samoan children. There was one little two year old called Sunya (Samoan for Junior). He was beautiful. His long black eyelashes and big brown eyes just captured my heart. It took awhile to win his confidence, but he let me hold and cuddle him. I couldn't help but think how wonderful it would be to have our own baby.

"Frank, do you ever think about us having more children?" I asked one morning over coffee.

"Yes, I do, but I wonder how we could handle our mission life with little kids," he contested.

"Ewen and Gillian did all right with Ruth and Michael," I pushed a little. "I really want to have a baby. Let's at least pray about it."

It didn't take God long to answer us on this one! The very next morning, Frank told me, "I feel like God has said a very strong 'Yes' to the baby."

Our decision to plan a pregnancy perfectly coincided with the fertile phase of my cycle. Or better yet, the Lord moved us to that decision at the perfect time. The night we conceived our second child, we felt the nearness of God. His presence filled our simple room and filled our happy hearts. *I knew He had given us a child from the very first moment. It was awesome!*

We had to make the bus trip into Pago Pago at least twice a week for groceries. There was also one English Mass every Sunday in town. One Sunday, as we were leaving Pago Pago on the bus, we spotted a large sign over one of the native Samoan houses not too far from the market. The sign said, "JESUS IS LORD!"

We were spiritually hungry for fellowship with others who boldly proclaimed the Lordship of Jesus. Longing to experience spirit-filled praise and worship motivated us to make a note of the location of that house. We decided to visit on our next trip to the Pago Pago.

As our bus whizzed by a few days later, we noticed, to our distress, that the "Jesus is Lord" sign was down. After shopping, we looked for the place anyway and came upon the sign, taken down from the roof but leaning against the house. The place was in total disarray, obviously being packed up for a move.

"Hello, anyone here?" we called out.

A nice looking young man about twenty-two years old came forward from behind the boxes. "Hi! Can I help you?" he asked.

"We're looking for some Christian fellowship on this island," Frank announced.

"Well, such as it is, you've just found it," he laughed as he offered us his hand. "My name is John."

Then he added, "There really are other Christians on this island, but right now I feel pretty lonesome. This is the American Samoan Youth With A Mission ministry. The ministry leader is in Guam on an outreach. I'm just house-sitting. It happens that the lease is up. We're supposed to move to another location."

He put his arm around Beau's shoulder, "Come over here to the office, it's still pretty intact, and tell me about yourselves."

We liked John a whole lot. He was humble and sincere, and full of the Lord! It was a pleasant surprise to find this mission base here in Samoa. He was excited to hear our testimony, and we were excited to hear his. John's sharing on Youth With A Mission especially impressed us. We spent two hours with him. It seemed like minutes.

Go! You Are Sent 172

As we got up to leave, he asked us if we needed anything from the building. They would be moving and were clearing out quite a bit. Frank spotted a yellow plastic Wesson Oil bottle that had "kerosene" written on it.

"Do you need that kerosene bottle? We have a small kerosene stove, and we have to go to the store twice a day with a Coke bottle to purchase kerosene."

"Take it, the new place we're renting has an electric stove. We won't be needing it."

He promised to visit us in Laulii the next day, and he did. We ate together, and then worshipped Jesus in song and prayer. The Holy Spirit was building brotherhood.

There was about an inch of kerosene at the bottom of the bottle John gave us from the YWAM building. I poured it into the little stove and figured it would last me about a day. I was surprised when two days later the stove lit again on that small amount of kerosene.

Incredulous, I went into the living room and said to Beau and Frank, "The Lord is multiplying that kerosene we got from YWAM. I'm still cooking on it."

John came back the next day with Jim Boetcher, one of the big supporters of the YWAM ministry in American Samoa.

The Federal Aeronautics Agency had a substantial operation on American Samoa, and several Christian families employed there were involved in the ministry. The Boetchers had a home in the compound on one end of the island, not far from the airport.

"You guys will like Dave Hall. He's the leader of the YWAM ministry. He'll be back soon," Jim said.

"Is he the one that's in Guam now?" I asked.

"That's him. Dave's been looking for a married couple for the new base of operations. A young lady and two other young men are coming to American Samoa to join the evangelism team. YWAM requires a married couple to be house parents when guys and girls are housed under the same roof."

"That's a wise requirement," Frank replied.

"Maybe your family is the answer to our prayer for house parents," Jim said hopefully.

He invited us to a meal and a prayer meeting at his home on the following Friday night. Barbara Boetcher cooked a great meal for us, but the fellowship and prayer were even better. That was the first time Frank played the guitar at a prayer meeting.

The idea of being house parents in an evangelistic ministry was appealing, and yet we had some reservations. We were Catholics and hadn't envisioned ourselves in an interdenominational ministry. We didn't know how we would respond to Dave, or he to us. Jim shared with us that YWAM was working with the Catholic nuns at a school further inland —so Catholics were included in the work.

We didn't want to get too excited about it, or turn it down, until we met and talked with Dave.

Meanwhile, Jesus was multiplying the kerosene. If I hadn't seen Him multiply food, I would have been unnerved by the miracle. Seven days had passed and I had not poured another drop of fuel into the stove.

"What are you trying to tell us, Holy Spirit?" I asked Him every time I cooked.

As each day passed we marveled more at the kerosene supply.

Finally, Dave returned to Samoa. John brought him to dinner to meet us. We felt an instant mutual respect.

Go! You Are Sent   174

"I agree with Jim. Your being here, waiting to find a ministry, might very well be the answer to our prayers for house parents," Dave told us over dessert.

"We'll seriously consider it and pray about it, and get back to you as soon as we hear what God wants," Frank assured him.

After the supper dishes were done, Frank and Beau called me into the living room. "Again, Lord Jesus, we come to you needing guidance. Do you want us to be house parents at the YWAM evangelism base? We offer ourselves to You if that is how You want us to serve You here in American Samoa," Frank prayed.

The three of us heard God's "Yes, do it." We quickly decided. We knew, surely, that YWAM was the reason Jesus had brought us to Samoa.

The month's rent was almost up. And so once we decided, it didn't take us long to move out of the house in Laulii to the YWAM base in Nu'uli. We cooked on that little bit of kerosene for SIXTEEN days. Much to our surprise, on the day we accepted Dave's offer, the kerosene ran out.

"Oh no," we worried.

"If the multiplication of the kerosene was a sign of Your blessing on our relationship with the Youth With A Mission people, Jesus, then why has it run out now?" we asked the Lord.

The answer came to us in our prayer time. We had been reading in the book of Exodus. The manna fell for the Israelites in the desert every day —a miraculous supply. But when they finally reached the promised land, the manna stopped. Did our kerosene supply last until we accepted the offer because YWAM was our "promised land" for now, here in Samoa?

We thanked the Lord for His faithfulness to lead us by signs and wonders, as He had done for His people since Bible times.

Straight evangelistic ministry suited us perfectly.

What we desired most was to tell the world the good news. As an evangelism team, ourselves and the longer term YWAMers, we found the source of strength and guidance for the ministry in our daily household prayer. Dave Hall, Phil Sylvester, Myron Musick, Debbie Smith, and the Summers family had some dynamite prayer sessions.

We heard the Lord tell us to go forth evangelizing in diverse ways. The team ministered in the prison, in the hospital, and in door-to-door visitation. We offered our services to the churches. We ran a Christian bookstore. (Beau was very blessed by the abundance of Christian books.) We conducted Bible studies in the house, sent out a newsletter, held weekly teachings and prayer meetings, and celebrated a weekly evangelistic covered dish supper called the "Love Feast".

During our time with YWAM, the Lord taught us a lot of important lessons. One essential lesson for family missionary life was that when the Lord prepares a place for us, that place is according to *His plan* for each member of the family. Not a single member of the family is ever short-changed in God's good plan.

Beau was eleven, and the YWAMers were young adults. He admired them and wanted to imitate them. He strongly desired to win their respect. We all fasted one day a week. As young as he was, Beau wanted to fast, too. The only problem was that our fast day was the day when Beau had the chance to go swimming with a friend his own age. He'd come back wiped out.

At times, I would try to persuade him to eat something light, but he usually refused. Perhaps he felt that if he broke the fast

Go! You Are Sent 176

he'd loose the respect of the others. At YWAM, Beau learned to go right to the heart of God in prayer and fasting. Still, I worried that he had taken on suffering that was too much for his years.

Nu'uli, the location of the base, didn't provide Beau with many neighborhood friends. Bureaucratic red tape prohibited us from putting him in the schools, and we agonized over his education.

One day in my prayer time, I was pouring my heart out to the Lord, expressing all my concerns about Beau. Tears flowed as I began to hear that familiar voice saying, "Genie, I chose this place not only for you and Frank. I chose this place for Beau. No lessons taught in school will ever be as valuable for him as living in close relationship with these 'on fire' young people. He's getting the best education he can possibly get at this moment."

As for the suffering, Jesus instructed me on that, "You and Frank, as parents, shouldn't try to protect your children from the cross. You should rejoice when your children have the courage to pick up their cross each day and follow me. I am building Beau's character as My disciple."

Frank received a word from the Lord about the same time, a word that has enabled us to travel about with our family, free to trust the Lord for their education.

The Lord said to Frank, "Trust Me, all wisdom and knowledge comes from Me. Beau's education is My responsibility. I can use schools, but I don't need them."

It was not easy to respond to that word. The false god of education has a stronghold in the American culture, and in many cultures in the world today.

Everywhere we went, after deciding to trust the Lord for Beau's education, we caught flack about it. We could see the

Lord educating Beau and making him a mature, capable young man. Everyone else thought we were crazy. Even dedicated Christians often made Beau feel as though we were failing him by not "staying put", so that he could go to school.

Years later, when he graduated as the Outstanding Graduate at the 100th Commencement of the University of Southwestern Louisiana, we saw the fulfillment of God's promise and our vindication. Beau had no formal high school training, he entered the University as an honor scholar and won thousands of dollars in scholarship and fellowship awards. In Pago Pago, we had no way of knowing about his future successes, but we had already come to know very well the Lord we served. All of Beau's needs would be met. We trusted that.

Our base and home in Nu'uli was a place of hospitality. Many Samoans came in and out like family. At the base, you could almost always encounter YWAMers in one-on-one ministry with our visitors. Two young Koreans (off a fishing boat) spent several days with us. I walked in from the grocery store one day, and found Phil and these two guys laughing naturally as though they were old friends. The Koreans didn't speak a word of English and we didn't speak a word of Korean. But, by using their Bibles to communicate, looking up Scripture passages, Phil and his new friends conveyed their messages to one another. Christian love is a universal language.

Frank loved prison ministry. It seems that there is an automatic grace in it. Jesus says, "I was in prison and you visited me."

In Samoa, prisoners were sometimes let out for the weekend or on holidays. The warden was pretty sure they couldn't get too far away on such a small island. Mikaeli was one of the prisoners that Frank had gotten to know. He came home with Frank one weekend, and was staying overnight. He and Beau slept in the same room. As I laid down that night next to Frank, I asked, "By the way, why is Mikaeli in prison? He seems like a very nice person."

Frank answered, "He's a convicted murderer."

I almost lost my breath. "Do you think Beau will be all right?"

"Sure I do, Mikaeli's had a deep experience of Jesus."

I must admit that I checked on them during the night. They were sleeping like babies.

The Love Feast was one of the highlights of our week. The YWAM team, the Boetchers, the Olsons, the Frenchs, and other Americans who supported and shared in our ministry joined together with our Samoan friends for teaching, praise, and worship, followed by a covered dish meal. We had guest speakers, or team members took turns giving teachings. Frank's preaching gift blossomed. The teachings were powerful. People responded with faith, called to a deeper walk with the Lord.

While we house parented the Nu'uli base, the love of Jesus and His Gospel was the center of our ministry. The fact that the Summers family was Catholic and the rest of the team was Protestant was an asset to God's work. We rejoiced in the diversity within our unity.

As time wore on, we could not extinguish the longing in our hearts to work more fully in the Catholic Church. We went back to the Lord in prayer.

"What should we do, Jesus? You know our hearts. We want to serve when, where, and how You want us to serve. But we are drawn to evangelism in the Catholic Church."

Two days later, we got a letter from Barry and Diane in New Mexico. It said, "The sense of community and the joy of the sacramental life out here in St. Bonaventure Mission is something to behold. We're living in service to the poor of New Mexico."

The letter was an answer to our prayer. We felt we should as least write and ask them if there was a place for us with them, even for a time.

YWAM was planning a big outreach. We spoke with Dave and it was agreed that if we left we should leave before the outreach started and not in the middle of it.

We wrote the Bordelons in New Mexico.

"Can the mission at St. Bonaventure use another family for a time? On our end here, we feel God is indicating New Mexico, what do y'all think?" Frank wrote candidly to Barry.

We considered it a minor miracle when Barry's reply arrived in only four days! Some letters had taken two weeks. Barry had talked it over with Father Doug McNeil, his pastor.

"Come as soon as possible," he suggested. "Can you make it by Christmas?"

Christmas was the busiest season of the year for air travel. The only flight out of Samoa with space available was on December 22. Our travel agent said the difficult part would be getting a confirmed flight from Hawaii to San Francisco to Alberquerque. We only had a couple of days if we were to make the December 22 flight.

"Lord, you be our travel agent," was our urgent plea.

Saying good-bye hurts. Through the years and across the miles, we still keep in touch with our YWAM friends.

Our tropical sojourn had mellowed and molded us. In Pago Pago, YWAM ministry had trained us in evangelistic mission outreach. But, the best blessing we carried away from our time in the islands was the new little missionary who witnessed to the Lord by its life in my womb. "Bless the Lord. Oh, my soul, bless the Lord. And let all that is *within me* bless His Holy Name."

Chapter Eighteen

Navajos to La Cueva

Being hugged by a band of Bordelons was the first installment of our Christmas gift.

"Genie, I like your little paunch. What do you think my godchild will be, a boy or a girl?" Diane asked.

"I hope it will be a little girl, like my new godchild," I answered grabbing the baby out of her arms.

Frank said. "Where's my godchild, Aaron?"

He's right here, Uncle Frank," Laurie Anne, Barry and Diane's oldest, said.

Father Doug welcomed us to the St. Bonaventure Mission. The Christmas Mass warmed my heart. Frank and Barry played guitars together. Father Doug fired us up with his message of hope.

The missioners had already arranged to share Christmas dinner with some Navajo families. Most of those families served the Parish. Still, a few were homeless, so were we.

Thoreau, New Mexico was our home for the holidays.

Jesus said, "When you give a feast, invite the poor..."

We prioritized deciding if the Lord would keep us in New Mexico or call us elsewhere. Several options opened to us there. A house was available at Blue Lake close to the Bordelon's home and ideal for building community. Or, if we were interested, Father Doug hoped that someone would establish a live-in ministry on the Navajo reservation.

Go! You Are Sent 182

The ancient, noble way of life on the reservation inspired us. We were drawn deeply to the privilege it would be to know them better. We knew that the more they embraced Christ, the keener would be their own ability to preach His word. How beautiful that word would be coming from such a rich heritage.

The Bordelons left New Mexico for a visit to Abbeville in late January and early February. We stayed behind on mission with Father Doug. Living in the mountains gave us a chance to be alone as a family. Barry had been right in his description of the mountains of New Mexico. They were beautiful in a spiritual way. God was near to us there.

St. Bonaventure mission was doing really admirable work. As much as we wanted the Lord to say clearly, "This is it. This is what I want you to do," we never heard it.

We begged God to show us His will.

We were led in prayer to write Father Rick Thomas, S.J. at Our Lady's Youth Center in El Paso, Texas. Another important thing God taught us in those early years, is that Jesus, the Lord of all the earth, is Lord of the *mail*. We didn't expect to get a quick response from Father Rick. We knew he had a pretty demanding apostolate to the poor.

He had preached at a day of renewal in New Orleans in 1974. There he boldly proclaimed that, "Just tithing doesn't fulfill the Christian's obligation , as it did in the Old Testament. A Christian is expected to give everything!"

"I could tell those were hard words for some to hear. But, I resonate with what Father Thomas is trying to tell us," Frank had said that day in New Orleans. By God's providence, we heard him just after we sold all of our possessions.

In the trailer at Blue Lake, New Mexico, we prayed we would receive a quick response from Father Rick; and the more we prayed, the surer we felt about serving the poor in the El Paso-Juarez area.

It surprised us to receive a personal invitation from Father Rick by return mail. Our hearts filled with gratitude as we decided to go forth to the Mexican people served by Our Lady's Youth Center. As usual, parting was tough, but at least El Paso was on the mainland.

Father Rick came to pick us up at the bus station. His eyes twinkled as he and Frank tossed our Tongan mat into the back of the truck. Here was an attorney turned missionary, his expectant wife, a twelve year old son arriving on a bus, with their few belongings wrapped in a Tongan mat. It was obvious we had heard from God the same word Father Rick lived and preached. We had given everything.

Beau rode in the back of the truck with "Fe", the dog.

How would the Lord fit our wandering little family of itinerant missionaries into an already established apostolate? God had something in mind, we had to find out.

On our first Saturday, we accompanied a van full of workers to the garbage dump in Juarez. Driving into the dump was a real shock. We were singing songs of praise, and the van was filled with the presence of the Lord! It seemed like a chariot from heaven driving through the outskirts of hell. Garbage was burning everywhere, black smoke rose up in eerie wisps. People moved slowly and listlessly through the heaps looking for valuable things like cardboard and aluminum cans. Little children were rummaging through the garbage looking for something to eat. Lean-to houses made of garbage, cardboard, mattress coils, pieces of tin, old blankets, and tarps were scattered about over the settlement.

Finally, up on a hill, a small chapel and school building came into sight. Up there was one faucet, where women were lined up to get water.

Near the hill, we drove up to the most decent house in the dump. It even had flowers and a small fence. The lady of the house came running out to the van with her Bible in hand, ready for the prayer meeting we would have on the hill.

"She's a new creation," Jeannie Soto, the driver of the van told us. "She's been touched by our ministry."

"Now she participates in giving catechism to the little children, " Mrs. Yañez, a new friend of ours, said.

"Did you hear about the Christmas miracle of the multiplication of the tamales and the ham? That's what started us reaching out on a regular basis to these brothers in the dump," Frank, one of the community members, inquired.

"When we first heard Father Rick in New Orleans, he told that story," I answered.

Frank from El Paso continued his explanation of the ministry, "Before the dump ministry began, there had been no source of water for all these families, except a truck that came sporadically. They were warring, imagine fighting over the garbage."

"Do you mean they had particular zones to glean the garbage?" my husband, Frank, asked our new friends.

"Exactly, the saddest part was the widespread tuberculosis, and the apathy that ravaged them," Jeannie said.

The church, now present through Our Lady's Youth Center, was a visible sign among these neglected outcasts of society. The dump ministry was founded on the teachings of Jesus. As the word of God took root in their lives, there was healing —physical healing and healing of relationships. The warring stopped. They formed a garbage gleaner union, they bought food, they rallied together and obtained a water line. Eventually, the Juarez government closed that dump, opened a new one and supplied housing on the *outside* of the dump so that no one had to live on the dump itself. God makes a difference.

Beau and Frank continued in the dump ministry for the duration of our stay in El Paso. They worked in the food store that sold the basics to the garbage gleaners at under-cost prices. Frank shared our testimony and teachings from the scripture through translators.

Father Rick had obtained permission to use the premises of the Holy Spirit Church in Juarez, Mexico for the first food bank. The Food Bank had been inspired by the scripture which says, "Anyone who does not work should not eat." (2 Thes. 3:10)

At the Food Bank, people in need of food or clothing would gather in the morning for singing, praising the Lord, and the proclamation of God's Word. This would be followed by individual prayers for physical healing.

Men and women would then be organized into work parties. The work parties would help rebuild streets, churches, or houses. The elderly women and the pregnant or nursing mothers stayed at the Holy Spirit Church and packed the beans, corn, and other groceries into family sized portions. Volunteers praised and sang while they prepared a hot meal for all the workers. The workers had a hot meal at the church, had their groceries distributed to them, and returned home to their families nourished and fed, both physically and spiritually.

Frank preached God's Word at the Holy Spirit Church food bank through the translation of Mrs. Tula. I saw cars stop, and people, hearing the preaching, leave their vehicles to seat themselves on the church steps with the crowd.

The Lord Jesus demonstrated that this work was His work. Miracles, signs and wonders were normal, expected events of each day. Mrs. Tula, myself, and a few others prayed over a woman with a withered hand, and by the end of the prayer, she had the hand held straight up in the air, completely healed.

One day, the evangelism team asked for a show of hands by those who had received physical healing. Hundreds were present, and there were only a few people that didn't lift their hands enthusiastically into the air.

Mr. and Mrs. Tula, were fully committed to the Youth Center ministry. Mr. Tula had been there for years, ministering to the young boys off the streets of Juarez and El Paso. He had been a great athlete himself, and had chosen the service of the Lord and His poor over a professional athletic career. Several years before, he had experienced a healing, a remission of cancer. By the time Frank and I met him, the cancer had returned to hurry Tula's service on this Earth to an end. He died shortly after we arrived in El Paso. He went to meet Jesus in Heaven.

My love of heaven must have started a long time ago. Dad told me that when I was a little girl, we were observing the stars together and I said, "Daddy, if the bottom of heaven is so beautiful, what must the top be like?"

The scriptures give so many analogies. In this life, we see in a "glass darkly." But in the life to come, we will see "face to face." I'm excited. I want to go to heaven. Of all the places the Lord prepares for us, heaven will be the absolute greatest!

I want to run the race to the finish. I want to wear the crown. I beg for the grace to be faithful, never to be ashamed of Jesus and His gospel, so that He won't be ashamed of me before His Father and His angels. The Lord gave me a vision once of God the Father dancing, and as He danced, the sun and the stars and all the heavens swirled happily in His cloak. He danced as on a day of joy. When it seems that the Christian life gets tough, I remember that we are being trained to bear the heavenly weight of glory, and I am strengthened.

Mr. Tula's funeral reinforced in my life this desire and hope for heaven. One of the nurses in the community told us that as Tula lay dying, the Holy Spirit came down on the whole hospital. The nurses station keyboard went crazy with calls from patients who wanted to find a priest for confession and ministry; many were weeping in repentance for their sins without really being aware of why they were feeling that way.

Mr. Tula had driven an old yellow Suburban van, transporting kids to various activities. Instead of a hearse, the yellow van was used to transport the casket.

Upstairs in the Youth Center, a faith filled wake was held. Songs of praise and thanksgiving filled the air. Of course, everyone grieved at the loss of their loved one, but "not like the pagans who have no hope."

The day of the funeral, the old cathedral was overflowing and songs of joy permeated the atmosphere. One by one, the children of this servant of God came up to the pulpit to bear testimony to the rich inheritance their father left them —a life of faith and hope in the living God! Mrs. Tula, even in the fullness of her pain, told of the security she felt about her husband being in heaven praying for those whom he left behind.

Frank led the young people in singing, "Tula's in heaven and he's walking with Jesus, Tula's in heaven and he sees His face, Tula's in heaven and he's walking with Jesus, saved by His wonderful grace." The government honored him with a twenty-one gun salute, and we sang the Battle Hymn of the Republic at the final send-off.

Go! You Are Sent 188

The whole group that met at the Youth Center, ourselves included, felt more like we'd been on a three day retreat than that we'd lost our friend.

One day, Father Rick called us into his office. Our Lady's Youth Center built a facility across the street from a large high school in El Paso. The facility was designed to minister to the vast majority of the students who were Mexican American. The school's mascot was the bear. The new building was called *La Cueva*. That's Spanish for "The Cave." Father Rick had been praying and waiting for the right brothers and sisters to operate this ministry.

Now, he was offering it to us. A brand new facility with an open door to operate in evangelism. Frank and I were honored by this vote of confidence.

"The building includes living quarters: three small bedrooms, a bath with a shower, a kitchen, and a laundry room. You could live and work there. Others will help you," Father Rick explained. "I think it should be spiritual ministry to the youth —Bible studies, prayer meetings, and fellowship."

"That sounds like the evangelism we're hoping for. Can I still participate in the Food Bank ministry?" Frank asked.

"Of course, and the garbage dump on Saturdays. You would model a radical gospel lifestyle. Very few of these youth see anything like that." Father Rick encouraged us to take the job.

At the Cueva, the busiest time of the day for us was lunch break. A constant stream of kids came in. We never had a meal without offering to share it with those around us. I began to cook large pots of soup, Cajun jambalaya, or any other meal I could think of that fed crowds of people.

The youth joined us for prayer, singing, then lunch. Some girls came faithfully to help me cook, and heat tortillas. We experienced again and again that multiplication of food. We never turned anyone away. In a short time, many young people were already regulars at the Cueva. There were the expected curiosity seekers, those who came only for the meal. But they, too, often ended up coming back after school for the Bible studies.

My pregnancy advanced, and we grew more excited about our new baby. In prayer one Saturday, we heard the Lord say for us to return to our home for the birth of our baby. It was a call we rejoiced in. I felt the need to rest more in the final three weeks of my pregnancy.

A young family, Ernest and Ester, agreed to take over the Cueva. Our testimony had inspired them to work full time for the Lord. The Lord had sent a family to fill our job —we were so excited.

"Father Rick, we feel a real desire to return home for the birth of the baby," Frank shared with Father.

We had been doing a lot of soul searching. If and when we returned to El Paso from Abbeville, we hoped to be a part of the Youth Center's ministry, but in Mexico.

"We'd like to live among the people in Juarez to learn their language and ways," Frank further explained our hopes.

Because we were able to pack up our belongings into our Tongan mat, it didn't take us long to be ready to go again. This time we were called to go back to Abbeville —to go with the gospel back into Cajun country.

Our send-off at La Cueva the eve of our departure was fantastic. The young people danced and sang and praised the Lord late into the night. Good-byes still weren't easy.

The big Amtrak train pulled powerfully out of the station in El Paso. We nearly broke our arms waving to our friends as we were whisked out of their sight. I breathed a big sigh of relief as I settled back into the comfortable seat, and found a foot rest. I needed to elevate my swollen feet.

Beau was soon bubbling with excitement at the prospect of seeing all of his grandparents again and his young aunts and uncles. A year and a half had passed since our departure for Tonga. Maybe Abbeville hadn't changed much, but we had lived a lifetime. God had tried us and tested us in our vocation. We had done quite a bit of wandering, and it didn't seem to be over yet. The light of the call to mission hadn't dimmed. It burned stronger than ever. Very few would understand. It didn't matter. We understood. We were unsure of the future, but sure of the call.

Chapter Nineteen

A Princess of Flowers

Soon we found a small apartment above Frank's grand-mother's garage. It was one of the poorest places we had lived in so far. We scrubbed and cleaned, but very little could be done to disguise the mismatched wallpaper and worn out linoleum. The redeeming feature was that it was up near the top of the trees. We were grateful to have a place to lay our heads.

"Well, one good thing about Mama Esther's garage apartment is that it's right here in the center of town," Frank commented.

"We can walk to church. That's good," I said. "We don't have a car."

"Mama Esther is one of my favorite people. I'll get to see her every day. That's what I like about it," Beau added.

"And don't forget, it's free. A gift," Frank said.

I sighed. "I guess we'll have to depend on our families and friends to take us to the grocery store. I don't think the baby will need air conditioning. We can get some fans."

It seemed we had so little time to gather the things together that we needed for our baby. A friend brought over a beautiful bassinet. I could picture our bundle of joy as I cleaned and readied it.

The other baby things that were in my family were fairly spread out. My sister, Rachel, was expecting their second baby. Bruce and Liz, my brother and sister-in-law, were expecting their second child. We called this bumper crop of Gremillion grand-babies, "the bicentennial bunch." It was a season of babies. We had bought a few baby clothes, but we didn't have quite enough. We didn't have the money to spend on an "all new" layette.

The time drew closer, and I continued to pray, "Lord Jesus, you always provide, don't forsake us this time." Two days before the baby was born, a cousin of Frank's arrived.

"Hi, Genie. The other day, I was going through my baby clothes and I thought maybe you could use some. I mainly brought girl clothes," Laura Lucia told me.

"This is an answer to my prayer, Laura. God must have sent you over here. Thank you," I answered.

"I'm happy to be the answer to prayer. If it's a girl, we'll be even more sure of that," she said laughing.

That was the most beautiful bundle of secondhand clothes I've ever received. Just the thought of dressing a tiny baby in all those frills blessed me beyond imagining.

Beau was spending the night with his grandparents, so Frank and I were alone when my labor started, five days before my due date. Frank had to borrow a vehicle to take me to the hospital. Jeannie Soto, my friend in El Paso, had given me some books on natural childbirth, as well as a few lessons. I had been practicing the relaxation techniques.

Frank sang, led us in the rosary, and read scripture to me during my labor at the hospital. He caressed me, held my hand, and helped me to relax.

We remembered Beau's birth. We had such a long wait, and neither of us had been able to witness the actual birth.

This birth was different. I was wide awake. Watching our first little girl come into the world was an awesome experience. Sarah Anthea came out screaming and crying.

When I asked the doctor, "Is she all right?"

Dr. Mayeaux answered, "That screaming baby! She's as healthy as can be."

She looked so pink and pretty. She had my mother's delicate nose and a little peach fuzz for hair. The family had gathered as we wheeled out of the delivery room.

"It's your first granddaughter, Mom," I told my smiling Mom proudly.

Beau and Frank were absolutely glowing. We kept extolling her beauty to one another. It was May 18, 1976. After all the visitors cleared out, we bowed our heads in humble gratitude. Now we were a family of four. The Lord had increased our numbers. A new missionary was dedicated to His service.

I was totally set on breast feeding our baby. In Tonga, Samoa, and Mexico, I had seen mothers breast feed their babies. In their cultures, it was the most natural thing in the world. And it is. Why did so few of my peers even consider it?

After a couple of days, Sarah began to show signs of jaundice. We worried.

"Discontinue breast milk. We'll put her under the bili-light (an apparatus in the incubator that heals the jaundice). She'll have to be blindfolded. The light's too strong for her eyes," The pediatrician informed me on Sarah's second day.

I was devastated. I cried.

"You and Frank have the RH factor blood incompatibility. Maybe she's getting antibodies through the milk."

After he left the room, I called out to the Lord, "Why am I having this problem, Lord? I believe nursing is the best possible thing for my baby. Help us, please."

Sarah was born on Tuesday night. On Thursday, due to the lack of funds, I could no longer remain in the hospital. I had

Go! You Are Sent 194

to leave her in the nursery under the bili-light. Memories of leaving another little baby long before, burdened me. Leaving her there was torture.

Friday night, I knew I couldn't be separated from our baby any longer. I prayed. I heard the Lord confirm what was in my heart. "You can take your baby home tomorrow. Call the doctor and tell him of your decision."

I felt tremendous peace as the still, firm voice once more showed me that His ways are above man's ways.

Saturday morning, I shared with Frank what I had heard the Lord speak to me during the night. He wholeheartedly agreed that we would take her home.

I phoned the hospital. "Doctor", I said, "I'm going to the hospital to bring the baby home, today."

"Oh, okay then, we'll do one more blood test on her before you get here to make sure she's out of danger."

We drove to the hospital as quickly as possible. I clutched Sarah to my heart. Soon she was nursing happily. Our newest missionary was right where she belonged.

Frank's Dad was still in New Orleans sitting on the Supreme Court. We named our beautiful new daughter, Sarah Anthea, after Sarah, the wife of Abraham and the mother of faith, and after St. Anthony, to fulfill a promise I had made to him long ago.

Judge Summers had visited the New Orleans public library to look up the etymology of the baby's name. He wrote us a lovely note saying that Sarah Anthea meant "Princess of Flowers". She was just that, a breath of spring that reigned in our hearts.

Frank was a very strong support to me as I began my new role as a nursing mother. I believe those first few days of separation from me, and the incubator stay, made Sarah feel insecure. Anyway, she cried a whole lot those first six weeks. Everyone had differing opinions, and didn't hesitate to tell me what they "knew" the problem was.

Most of the opinions had to do with breast feeding. Some said my milk was too strong, others said my milk was too weak. Some said I was feeding Sarah too often, others that I was not feeding her often enough.

"Why don't you just give her a bottle and see?" was the constant refrain from well-meaning friends and relatives.

The pressure others put on me in the area of nursing my baby was certainly something that I could approach the Lord about. I had learned that nothing that concerns me is insignificant to Him. I prayed about my discouragement and the Lord told me, "Genie, just imagine that you are in the jungle somewhere with no bottle, that baby would need your milk."

A nursing baby is very portable, especially in combination with disposable diapers. Frank and I began to be fully engaged in the Lord's service. Assuming again the responsibilities of parenting an infant renewed our longing for community. Beau was the best big brother, our family looked with expectant faith at our little girl's future life as a Christian.

We had several invitations to share our testimony, and to give teachings in prayer groups and Pre-Cana courses. Repeatedly, the brothers and sisters who wanted to live the gospel sought us out to talk about building a community in Abbeville. We hoped the Lord would build a community that had a heart for the missions. Our hopes were not realized. Abbeville was not yet prepared to support a community of itinerant lay missionaries.

One evening, Beau was downstairs visiting with Mama Esther, Sarah was sound asleep and a cool breeze was blowing through the apartment. We had come back from giving our testimony at a "Come Lord Jesus" couples group. The supper dishes were washed and I put the leftover crawfish étouffée away in the refrigerator. Frank and I were talking over a cup of coffee. We had so much to be grateful for, and yet, the urgency of our call to the missions impelled us to begin to plan where we would "Go!" next in the service of the gospel.

"I talked to Marylin and Joe Stark the other day. They're still waiting for us to come back to El Paso," Frank answered.

"Do you think we'll be able to live in Mexico, this time?" I asked.

"Joe thought Father Rick might be open to that," Frank said.

"There's another family in the Cueva, where can we stay in the meantime? The baby might be a problem for some people," I asked.

"Marylin and Fran invited us in the interim. They're anxious to see the baby," Frank assured me. Marilyn, Fran and Mary Beth loved their hospitality ministry. They had a neat place, the community in El Paso was blessed to have them.

We made our train reservations, cleaned our little apartment and moved into Mom and Dad's camp at Kisinoaks that overlooked the Bayou. It was air conditioned, had a pool, phone, lovely decor, the setting was perfect. That's where Frank and I had started out, on the Bayou. It would be only a few days. We planned to arrive in El Paso, and seek out our new ministry on the Juarez side of the border.

The day before the train was to depart for Texas, we received a phone call from our friends —Mary Beth had suffered a heart attack!

They would not be able to receive us until she was better.

"Well, Lord," Frank said in prayer, "Thank you for the clear sign. You have closed a door. It wasn't clear that You wanted us to return to El Paso. But, what now, Lord?"

"Please show us what Your will is for our lives." I pleaded with the Lord.

We knew the value of daily fellowship with other Christians. The book of Acts in the Bible was, for us, our handbook and inspiration in our missionary life. It also spoke to us of the community aspect of the Christian life. Some friends in Abbeville told us about the Alleluia community in Augusta, Georgia.

Frank wrote the Alleluia community asking if we could visit them. In the letter, he shared some of our testimony, and our desire to be in mission. He also expressed our sense of need to be in community. We received no response for two or three weeks.

A missionary can usually live in a third world country much less expensively than he can in the States. We were low on funds again. Frank went out to work, mowing pastures on his parents' farm. It was a very low ebb in our walk with the Lord. Even our daily prayer time seemed dry.

At least ten times in the Psalms, the psalmist cries out to God asking Him,

Why do you hide your face from me?
Hear, O Lord, and have pity on me,
O Lord, be my helper.

Psalm 30:11

The Psalm continues in verses 12 and 13; the answer had already come to the Psalmist:

You changed my mourning into dancing; you took off my sackcloth and clothed me with gladness. That my soul might

Go! You Are Sent 198

sing praise to you without ceasing; O Lord, my God, forever
will I give you thanks.

The ups and downs of the Christian life and the missionary
life were age old problems. There had always been mountains
and valleys, tears and rejoicing.

The Summers missionaries needed to have our mourning
changed into dancing. One afternoon, Frank came in sweaty
and tired from the farm. I had a pretty rough day with the baby.
Beau was feeling a little dejected because he wanted to talk to
his Dad, but Frank was just too tired.

"Why didn't you wear your cross today, Daddy?" he asked.
(We all wore wooden crosses on a string around our necks.)

"I don't know, Son," he answered, sighing, "I guess I don't
feel much like a missionary right now. I feel bad about the Lord
not showing us what to do next. Maybe He doesn't want us to
continue in mission."

Beau and I looked at each other and raised our eyebrows.
"Lord, you have to do something," I prayed under my breath.

I sat down to nurse the baby, and my Daddy came walking
up to our door with a letter for us. He walked in, invited us to
supper later, and handed us the letter.

"It's from the Alleluia Community in Georgia," I said
excitedly.

Frank tore open the envelope, and read the contents out loud
to us. Dennis McBride, an elder in the Alleluia Community,
had written us a beautiful letter, inviting us to visit their
community. "Come as soon as you like," the letter said. "Let
us know the time of your arrival. We look forward to your
visit."

All heaven broke loose on the bayou that day. We knew *this*
was the next step. This was the guidance we had been waiting
for. Frank and Beau danced around singing "Alleluia." They

A Princess of Flowers

changed into their swim trunks, ran out to jump into the pool, still shouting praises to the Lord.

We phoned Dennis early the next morning, telling him of our travel plans. We would take a train as far as Atlanta, and then travel by bus to Augusta. We would probably arrive in the middle of the night.

"Don't worry, someone will be there to pick you up," he told us.

The train ride was wonderful. Sarah was as good as a little angel. It felt good to be moving again, to go forth, sure that we were being guided by the Holy Spirit. Our family and personal prayer was vibrantly alive again. We had no idea, really, what the purpose of our time in Augusta would be, but we were convinced that Jesus had plans for us.

Twelve years after our train trip to Augusta, the Pope would say to a community of families in mission, "The Holy Family of Nazareth..was most of all an itinerant family, because it went everywhere...everywhere as itinerants to bear witness to the mission of the family, to the divine mission of a human family. I think that you as itinerant families... are doing the same. The goal of your journeying is to bring everywhere, in the various environments, perhaps into the most de-christianized environments, the witness of the family's mission.

"In this entire world, there is not a more perfect, more complete image of God, Unity and Community. There is no other human reality which corresponds more, humanly speaking, to that divine mystery. Therefore, as itinerants taking your testimony that is proper to the family, to the family on mission, you take where ever you go, the witness to the Most Holy Trinity on mission." (Pope John Paul II, Feast of the Holy Family address to the Neo Catechumenical Communities, December 30, 1988, Porto San Giorgio.)

Go! You Are Sent

In 1976, we didn't have the consolation of these encouraging words of the Holy Father. But we trusted.

There were other words to encourage us about being "itinerant," words not of the future, but words two thousand years old:

As they were proceeding on their journey, someone said to Him, "I will follow you where ever you go." Jesus answered him, "Foxes have dens, and birds of the sky have nests, but the Son of Man has nowhere to rest His head." (Luke 9: 57-58)

Chapter Twenty

Alleluia to Albermarle

Faith Village in Augusta, Georgia, was the site of community activities and of the Alleluia life lived in common. The village had been built by the US Army to house the married servicemen during the Korean war. It had later been sold and was being used as rental property. Several community families had bought houses, and others were renting.

The simple Christian homes were a wonderful witness to Jesus. We were housed in their guest house. They called it the ARC — Alleluia Retreat Center. The back doors of the houses all opened onto a common ground shaded with big pecan trees. There was a fenced playground, with children and babies by the score. We were living in a village of Christians — it blew my mind.

The first afternoon we were there, our whole family took a walk around the village. Later that night, Steve Swenson, a community member, came by the ARC to talk with us.

"I just wanted to congratulate you, Frank, on the order of your family. It is obvious from the way you handle yourselves."

What a welcome! This community blessed and upbuilt us and one another with their speech. The community was still young in 1976, but they learned important lessons in the formative stages. For Christians to live in unity, the manner in which you speak to or about one another is crucial.

Community members came to the ARC in the morning to cook breakfast for us and other visitors. During the first week, we were invited to share meals with different community families. Our sponsor family, the Vinsons, took us under their wing and saw that all our needs were met.

Since Alleluia is an ecumenical community, once again we enjoyed the company of brothers and sisters of different walks. The life they lived together in Faith Village was electrified with love.

We were in the ARC two weeks. After that, we moved into one of the community houses. The McArdles were going to Florida and they offered us their home. We were able to live the community life fully for a whole month. Seeing Christian community in action, was good for all of us. Sarah settled down and became a model nursing baby —a real "princess".

"What's happened to Sarah? She's so peaceful," Frank asked me one afternoon as we strolled her around the village.

"I'm surrounded by so many mothers who are happily nursing their babies. I think Sarah can sense that I'm more relaxed."

"Beau is flourishing here, too. He's found boys his own age who understand his commitment to the Lord," Frank said. "I'd say you're enjoying working with the men of the community repairing houses. It must be rewarding to make these homes ready for the constant influx of families from all over the nation."

"I'm getting to be a pretty decent drywall man," he laughed.

The Holy Spirit hovered "like a dove" over the whole place and over all their gatherings. Sharing with others about our call and commitment to mission life was exciting.

Because everyone else there had come by the leading of God's Holy Spirit, our itinerant odyssey found acceptance and interest. Their testimonies filled us with faith. God had brought many of them here on sheer faith.

The community had an outreach to the Army base near Augusta. They had a coffee house ministry for soldiers every week-end.

Frank was invited to play the guitar and tell the story of our call and conversion.

Beau had decided not to come with us, but to stay behind in the village with his friends. Harriet and Dennis McBride offered to keep an eye on him. Frank was almost finished with his presentation at the base, when I was called out of the club to the telephone.

It was Harriet. She said, "Beau has been hurt. Can y'all please come home?"

"She's pretty sure he's broken his arm," I told Frank as we drove back to the Village. "They need us to go to the hospital with him to sign the release for x-rays and any other procedures."

As we drove, we prayed. "We beg You, Lord Jesus, to heal Beau."

When we got to Harriet's house, a crowd had gathered. Beau was pale, yet composed. You could tell he had been crying a little.

"They were playing 'king of the mountain' on those big tractor tires out there," Dennis explained. "Beau fell down, all the boys heard a crack, and Beau screamed out in pain."

"We called Kent Plowman (Kent was a medical doctor in community) and put Beau's arm in a sling. He's sure it's broken," Harriet, explained.

"Thank the Lord, it wasn't his neck," I said.

"Did y'all pray over him?" Frank asked.

"We did that first," Dennis said, "but he's still in pain."

We went up to hug Beau; he was very protective of his arm. Any slight movement caused him excruciating pain.

"Kent and his wife, Diana, will be here in a minute to go with y'all to the hospital. Tonight's their date night. They went home to dress for dinner after Kent sets Beau's arm", Harriet told me.

We made Beau sit on the sofa with us and we prayed again over the injured arm. Beau winced and groaned if we barely touched his arm.

"Do you have any Holy Oil?" Frank asked Dennis.

One of the McBride children went for the can of Holy Oil, but we couldn't get it open.

Frank said, "I really feel the Lord wants to heal Beau, let's pray again." We prayed again.

"Daddy, it still really hurts! It hurts a lot!" Beau said, almost crying.

"Kent and Diana are here," someone called out.

"I want to pray for him with Holy Oil before we take him to the hospital," Frank insisted.

I volunteered, "I'll go next door and get ours."

I ran over and came back quickly with the Holy Oil we had brought with us from El Paso. Everyone was getting a little impatient as Frank unscrewed the bottle of Holy Oil and started to pray for the third time.

"Father, please heal our son," Frank prayed simply, and then anointed Beau's arm, making the sign of the cross with the oil.

Suddenly, Beau whipped his arm out of the sling and began jumping and shouting, "I'm healed! Praise you, Jesus, I'm healed!"

The whole crowd broke into applause and laughter to see Beau jumping around. Diana locked her arm into Kent's and said, "Thank you, Lord, for my sake, too. Now Kent and I can go on our date."

While we were there, my sister gave birth about a month early to her daughter, Jennifer. They called us right away. Jennifer's lungs were not sufficiently developed. She was in serious danger. She was struggling for every breath.

Noon prayers at Faith Village flew directly to heaven. Everyone gathered around for singing, praising, and petitions. The charismatic gifts operated. Prayers were answered. I told Rachel on the phone not to worry.

"You have your baby baptized, and I will bring your petition to noon prayers. Call me back tomorrow and let me know how she is."

When I finished offering up the prayer for the healing of Jennifer, someone declared that they heard the Lord say, "It is done. Your prayers are answered."

The next news I got from Rachel was that Jennifer was showing immediate improvement. They didn't need to transfer to another hospital. She had been baptized. The doctors were confident that soon she would be out of danger.

Our little family felt very drawn to the community life at Alleluia. We expressed this attraction to the leaders at that time: Bill Beatty, Dennis McBride, Dale Clark and Kevin Murrell. Frank spent several hours with them together, and separately, discussing the ways and means of handling our call to missions in light of our desire to be a part of the community.

As deeply as they respected our call to mission, they were asking us to lay aside that call, become members of Alleluia, and dedicate our energies to the further building of the community. They suggested Frank re-enter the practice of law, because the community needed a lawyer. And if, at some future date, the community felt a call to missions, we could submit our desire to go forth again.

We were torn, drawn to the wonderful life they were building together. However, our hope had been to become members of the community as missionaries. We wanted to fulfill our calling and bless the community by our mission.

The Vatican II document on the missionary activity of the church declares that a home community or church will be blessed in proportion to its generosity in sharing the good news with those far off —in mission. Peace eluded us when we thought of putting aside our call to mission.

In the end, we decided we needed to move on, to go again. The co-ordinators invited us to stay on indefinitely as their guests, and as "a prophetic witness to the community." We very much appreciated the heartfelt offer, but we knew the longer we stayed, the more difficult it would be to leave.

We would carry the good news of the Alleluia Community with us to the ends of the earth. Everywhere we ever went we told the stories of God's good servants in Augusta and Faith Village.

Bill Beatty brought us to board another bus. Our itinerant family was on the go again.

The Lord knew Frank's brother and his wife would invite us to house sit for them while they traveled. Jesus had planned months in advance to provide a temporary home for us with a garden that was ready to harvest. When they planted, they didn't realize that they would be away and that we would be the ones to eat its produce.

Albermarle County, Virginia is a beautiful, scenic, picture-postcard kind of place. Tucked away in a hidden corner of the county is a humble "holler" called Brown's Cove. In Faith

Village, the Lord had given us an experience of the joys and difficulties of Christian community. In the small two story wood frame house here in Brown's Cove, the Lord taught us other important lessons. Lessons for the quiet seasons of our life in mission. We moved in Him, in His grace, to a time of solitude.

The little house was on a small river about seventeen miles outside of Charlottesville, in a wooded area. We had a week's visit with Jim and Kathy before they left and we got our "bearings" on the surroundings. Once they left, we were out in the country without a vehicle and with no near neighbors. A mile down the road, there was a little country store.

We ate very simply and very well, with many different kinds of vegetables (turnip soup was one of our favorites). I made lots of tortillas, using a Pepsi bottle for a rolling pin. Beau became an expert at baking cornbread.

The nearest Catholic church was in Charlottesville, seventeen miles away. St. Thomas Aquinas Parish that served the University of Virginia was alive and well. Even though we had no car, missing Sunday mass never occurred to us. We hitchhiked, and that became one of the most fruitful "outreaches" we've ever had. We stood alongside the shady country road that wound over the hills. Even as we waited for a ride we could hear the bubbling of the river. We had to start early, we were uncertain of how long it would take.

Most cars whizzed by without looking back. We prayed as each car approached, asking God a ride. Our witness blessed those who accepted the Lord's prompting to pick us up. There were several families who not only gave us a ride to church, but gave us rides after Mass as well.

The Lord chose generous people. They had to have courage to make room in their car for a unique family, wearing crosses.

Frank dressed in Sears work clothes and sported a full beard. I carried four month old Sarah in a kangaroo-carry front pack, and, at that time, was still wearing long dresses that I'd adopted in Tonga. Beau, a tow headed twelve year-old dressed in old Levis was the only typical American in the group.

We made some wonderful friends. They came for meals. We were invited into their homes. We had many opportunities to pray and share Jesus with the Christian folks who lived in and around Brown's Cove.

Frank also had to hitch rides into town once or twice a week to buy groceries and supplies. He began by begging the Lord, "Let the person most in need of Your love stop to pick me up. Prepare him to receive Your Word through me, and give me what You want him to hear."

Frank always returned with reports of the ways the Lord worked in his trip to town. He openly prayed with drivers for healing, deliverance, and conversion.

One day, after one of Frank's trips into town, a young man named John Finley drove him home. John greeted us warmly. He seemed friendly, yet a little uncomfortable. We invited him to stay for dinner, but he declined. He'd really gone out of his way to take Frank all the way back home.

We invited him to come back and he answered, "I might just do that."

I doubted it; we lived about ten miles from his home. Two days later, I was taking a little pack of meat out of the freezer for dinner. I heard the Lord say to me, "Take two packs out, someone is coming for dinner."

I argued with Him. "Lord, if I take two packs out we'll eat it all, and then we'll be short a days worth of meat for the week. I hate for Frank to have to go back into town to buy more supplies."

"Take two packs out, *and* cook more potatoes *and* make a bigger salad," the Lord insisted.

I obeyed, and shared what the Lord said with Beau and Frank.

I was putting dinner on the table and still no one had shown up. "Well, I'll just try to save the leftovers for tomorrow," I thought. "Maybe the Lord's people decided not to come." All of a sudden, there was a knock on the back door. John Finley stuck his head in, asking, "May I come in?"

"Sure," I replied, "As a matter of fact, I was expecting you. The Lord told me we were having company for dinner and I've prepared enough. You'll just have to join us."

He smiled a little, "I would enjoy a family meal. It smells good in here."

Beau came running out of the living room where he'd been reading, and gave John's hand a vigorous shake. "It's that cornbread that smells so good. I made it."

"Frank," I called out, "John Finley is here, and dinner is on the table."

We were all really glad to have company; it sometimes got a bit too isolated. We had a lively conversation. John came from a very Christian family. His parents lived in Brazil where they were administrators in the World Health Organization, in Sao Paolo. John had lived in Africa. We felt a kindred spirit with him right away.

As the meal ended and we spread the last homemade preserves on our cornbread, John said, "The real reason that I've come here tonight is that I want to give my life to Jesus Christ."

A solemn silence fell as he continued, "I was raised in an evangelical Protestant home. I followed the Lord as a child; but in growing up, I grew away from Him, rejecting and ignoring my upbringing. So many things have happened to me in the last year to remind me that He still has a plan for my life."

We listened intently as he went on with his story, "I fell off a mountain while rock climbing. It was a miracle that I survived with only minor scrapes. Then my truck went off the road over a deep drop-off and was caught by a tree that protruded from the mountainside. I knew the Lord was trying to get my attention," he continued shaking his head.

"Then the other day, when I picked you up, Frank, everything you said went straight to my heart. You seemed to be sorting things out and setting my mind straight. I went home to think about it. This might sound kind of funny, but I thought, 'These Catholics are really sold-out to Jesus and His Word. I'd better move with this opportunity and come back to the Lord!' I want to give my life to Him. Will y'all pray for me?"

We all gathered around and placed our hands on his shoulders. John came back to the Lord Jesus. There was rejoicing in heaven!

We found out why they called these coves in the hills of Virginia, "hollers". A few of the inhabitants did "holler" back and forth across the valleys and hills. We heard the sounds of arguing and cursing. We heard shotguns firing, and children screaming. The noises were not happy noises but sounds of disorder and turmoil.

We prayed for these families daily. One morning after an especially noisy night in the holler, Frank sat on the back porch praying the Liturgy of the Hours, and then decided to pray an exorcism over the whole valley.

He used the "Prayer against Satan and the Rebellious Angels," published by Order of His Holiness Pope Leo XIII. "The Holy Father exhorts priests to say this prayer as often as possible, as a simple exorcism to curb the power of the devil and prevent him from doing harm. The faithful also may say it in their own name, for the same purpose, as any approved prayer. Its use is recommended whenever action of the devil is suspected, causing malice in men, violent temptations and even storms and various calamities."

It was a cool, almost cold Autumn day. All of our doors and windows were shut. Frank came directly in to eat after his prayer against Satan. The food was on the table.

As we stood singing our customary song of praise and blessing the food, the room began to fill up with *flies*. Not small black flies, but big green, shiny flies. At first, there were about fifty, then one hundred, then about five hundred; and more kept appearing. We were acutely aware that something weird was going on. The strangest thing was that they could not land on us. They couldn't land on our food. It was as though there was an invisible shield about two to three inches above the table and around us.

Some of the flies were banging themselves against the windows and falling down dead. Some kept buzzing around. We couldn't eat. We knew that even if we used insect spray it wouldn't do any good. There were just too many!

"What are we going to do?", I asked Frank.

"Yeah, this is pretty gross, and I'm getting hungry," Beau said.

"I don't see how we can eat in the middle of this," I said.

"I was just reading in the footnotes of the Jerusalem Bible the other day that *Beelzebub* means 'the lord of the flies'. The devil must be angry at your prayer, Dad. Real angry," Beau commented.

Go! You Are Sent 212

Frank shook his head in agreement, "Right, Son. I'm going to get the Bible and we'll read some Psalms. You get the Holy Water."

Frank went around the house sprinkling Holy Water, and then he sat down at the table and started reading the Psalms. As he read the Psalms, flies flew into the windows and walls and died. Then Frank opened the door and the rest flew out.

Relieved and impressed at the power of God's Word, we thanked the Lord for His protection, then sat down to eat our cold meal. We spent some time after lunch sweeping up piles of flies. None had fallen on our table or on us.

Jim and Kathy were coming home. Our house-sitting time was up. In prayer, we remembered meeting Ralph Martin in Fiji. We decided to take this opportunity to accept the invitation he had made to us to "visit the Word of God Community any time."

In Ann Arbor, we hoped Ralph could direct us to Charismatic clergy in developing nations that needed a family of lay missionaries. We also looked forward to seeing him again and meeting his family.

John Finley drove us to the bus station in Washington, D.C. to catch a bus to Ann Arbor.

"Thanks for everything, John," Frank said as they shook hands.

"My pleasure. Call me when you come back to Brown's Cove."

Chapter Twenty One

Rescue

"Ann Arbor was gorgeous, wasn't it? The fall was almost as colorful as Cape Cod. Bob and Shari Wild wanted us to join the community, don't you think?" I asked Frank.

"They were certainly very open to us, and their hospitality was terrific. I didn't hear God telling us to stay there, but I'm glad we have connected with them. I think it will be important in the long run," Frank said.

"I liked the music ministry at the Word of God Community, and the Wild family," Beau said.

"Do you think anything will come of the information Ralph gave us about the priest in Colombia?" I asked Frank.

"I plan to write to him as soon as possible. I felt very good about that," Frank answered.

"All aboard for St. Louis," the voice on the speaker in the Chicago train station crackled.

"Let's go! I'm tired of waiting around," Beau said.

We situated ourselves on the train. It pulled out of Chicago. We had heard the Lord tell us to head South again. Our next stop was St. Louis, Missouri. We hoped to spend a few days checking out possibilities for ministry. Because we didn't know a single person there, our plan was to rent a room for a few days.

"Do you feel God leading us to St. Louis, Frank?"

Go! You Are Sent
214

"Not especially, I just feel that it's worth looking into, this is a crossroads. It might be a place to minister until Latin America opens for us."

I'm disappointed that we haven't been able to tie up with a community. Religious missionary orders have done it for centuries," I said to Frank.

"Maybe the Holy Spirit doesn't want that yet for our lives. Missionaries are like the blood in the blood stream. They bring the good news from one community to another," Frank answered.

Beau loved exploring each new train. He always came back from his exploits with reports of interesting acquaintances he had made with travelers of all ages.

The train was scheduled to arrive in the early evening and was completely filled. About four hours out of St. Louis, the train stopped.

"There's been a freight accident down the track," I heard a passenger say.

"The porter told me we'll be delayed another several hours. This is so irritating," her companion replied.

An Amtrak official came into the car where we were seated and announced, "Buses will be provided for those who need to be on their way. We will be boarding the buses out of the next car."

Much to our surprise, almost all the passengers cleared out.

We had our baby, Sarah. And we didn't have any deadlines. So we decided we'd just relax.

"Let's take advantage of the quiet, enjoy the rest and stay on the train," Frank suggested.

"Sounds good to me," I said.

Another couple with a small baby stayed on also. The father was a soldier. That was it, except for the crew. We had the whole train to ourselves. Frank took out his guitar. We went to the club car. It was very comfortable. We sang and praised the Lord. Beau had already befriended and witnessed to the crew, who gave us bag lunches for our dinner.

"No doubt about it, families make a good team for mission," I thought.

We felt pretty good about our decision to remain on the train.

We got moving again at about 10:00 p.m. and slept fairly well with the rocking motion. We were all awakened as we pulled into the station at 2:00 a.m. Shortly after we detrained in the St. Louis station, the whole crew cleared out and went home. Only the soldier and his wife and baby were with us in the deserted station. The station was enormous. It reminded me of a scene from a movie set at the turn of the century. Our footsteps and voices echoed in the huge empty building.

We found chairs about half a city block from the telephone booths and sat down, while Frank went upstairs and out to the street level. He hoped to get a taxi to take us to a hotel, or even spot a hotel within walking distance.

After a while he came back.

"It's real dark and deserted out there. It looks like a part of town you wouldn't want to go walking around in at two o'clock in the morning," he reported.

"This station doesn't look much better, there's not even a night watchman. It gives me the creeps, " I shuddered.

"What? We're not going to a hotel? I'm really sleepy," Beau grumbled.

Go! You Are Sent 216

"If it's okay, I'll see if I can phone a hotel or something, and when we have reservations we can phone a taxi," I said. "Beau, keep an eye on Sarah. She's asleep."

I first tried calling rooming houses. Either the owners were angry for being awakened, or the "rooming houses" were really brothels. It was a wipe-out.

I came walking briskly back to where Frank, Beau and little Sarah were. The soldier and his wife were seated a few rows in back of us.

"Nothing, nothing," I said, shaking my head in frustration, "Why don't you try?"

Frank walked over to the telephone booth. I nursed Sarah back to sleep and put her into her little carry-bed. I could see Frank looking up number after number in the phone book. He had his back turned to us as he talked. He didn't appear to be having any success.

Suddenly, I was startled by running footsteps. They sounded like thunder. I turned around to see a young man come running up to us. He wore tight blue jeans and a polo shirt. He was very muscular, a body builder. He had a short, sandy, blond, clipped haircut. His eyes were glazed, but he didn't smell like he had liquor on his breath. He was hyped-up and turned to me frantically, "I gotta get out of here, I gotta get out of here!"

Stepping closer toward me, he shouted, "When is the next damn train out of here?"

I was terrified by then, because I spotted a rubber mask hanging out of his back pocket, the kind of grotesque mask that covers the whole head!

"That's the kind of mask they use in violent crimes," I thought desperately.

Chills ran up and down my spine. I began to call out to the Lord in my heart and to pray in tongues under my breath.

"When is the next damn train out of here!" he shouted, again emphasizing his question with curses and profanities.

Beau suddenly became very upset. This worried me too. I looked over at Frank in the phone booth. It seemed like he was ten miles away! He still had his back turned, unaware of our distress.

The soldier stood up and I sat down.

The crazy guy sat down next to me. I scooted over in my chair. Beau sat down next to him and said, "We're Christians and we don't like cursing. Besides, we don't know when the next train leaves."

This made him even angrier, "I wasn't talking to you, Buddy. I was talking to her, and don't you bother me again, you little..."

I interrupted him, saying excitedly, "Look over there, there's the ticket booth. Can't you see it? It looks like the next train out is at 6:15 in the morning. It goes to New Orleans."

This distraction worked for a few seconds as he tried to read the posted scheduled.

"New Orleans. I could go to New Orleans, but I can't wait till no six o'clock in the morning." This, too, was emphasized by profanities.

He glared at Beau. "I know all about Christians, you don't have to tell me about Christians! I know every damn thing there is to know about Christians!"

Then he reached for his back pocket and took our several worn Gospel tracts. "What do you think of this? It says, 'For God so loved the world that He gave His only son that we might not die, but have eternal life.'"

Trying not to cry, I said, "That's right. That's what Jesus did, He died for us."

Go! You Are Sent 218

About that time, Frank walked up. He could tell something was wrong. The guy was sitting there with the Gospel tracts in his hand. That should have been something positive. But, he could read our faces. We looked very afraid.

Evidently, this fellow had not seen Frank in the phone booth, and he thought that Frank was someone coming in from the outside. He threw his arm around the back of my chair and caught hold of my shawl.

"I'm with her, I'm with her!", he said desperately.

Frank grabbed my hand and pulled me up to his side.

"I'm with them," the guy said pointing to Beau and the soldier's family.

"What's going on here?", Frank asked. The guy jumped to his feet. "What's it to you?" He raised his voice and shook his fist! "Who the hell do you think you are?"

Then he called Frank a string of filthy names.

At that exact moment, the doors to the terminal parking lot swung open. In walked a very tall, handsome black man. His clothes were immaculate. His plaid sports coat, white shirt, silk tie, navy pants, and highly polished shoes were in exquisite taste. He walked purposefully over to us.

"Wow, His footsteps don't echo," I thought.

"Do you people need a ride?" he asked in a calm, authoritative voice.

The crazed body builder said again, "I'm with them!"

The black man looked sternly at him, and the guy backed off and shut up.

The soldier and his wife immediately said, "Yes, we'll take a ride."

Frank was still baffled. "I don't know," he said.

Beau pulled urgently on his arm, "Let's go with him, Dad."

Rescue

"Let's take this ride, ple-e-e-ese Frank!" I was trembling with fear.

Frank looked our rescuer in the eyes, he was convinced it would be okay. "Thanks, we'll take the ride," he said.

The man in the sports coat began to help us carry our luggage.

The guy with the mask ran along behind us, shaking the Gospel tracts at us and shouting profanities. But he stayed clear of our rescuer.

Our escort turned around and crisply told him, "Get out of here."

The Bully took off running. He ran out of the station and down the street.

We walked out to a car parked in the dimly lit parking lot. As we walked, Beau and I were bombarding Frank with details of what had taken place.

"Frank, I've never experienced the nearness of dangerous evil like I did when that guy lit into Beau," I explained.

The black man's car was a black Cadillac. As we got in and drove away from the station, I breathed an enormous sigh of relief. We began to tell the driver all about ourselves and about the terrible scare we'd had.

The soldier and his wife opened up. "I felt helpless. I was torn between running upstairs and out of the building for help or trying to distract him. I couldn't come up with a plan that made sense in light of the two babies," the soldier said.

"I was just plain scared to death," the wife said.

We drove out of the train area and headed out onto an expressway. "Where are we going?", Frank asked.

"I'm taking you to a motel on the interstate," the driver answered confidently.

Go! You Are Sent 220

I was no longer *afraid*. In fact, I felt *rescued* —God's peace was in this automobile! "I love you, Lord," I whispered.

We drove up to a Holiday Inn on the outskirts of St. Louis, brought our luggage in and were greeted by the night desk clerk.

"We have one room left," he said. "How did you know about it? There's a huge convention in St. Louis, and this is the last room available in the whole city!"

The black man shook Frank's hand and walked out to his car. I quickly asked Frank, "How much did you pay him?"

"He wouldn't let me pay him anything. He wouldn't take money."

"Oh, Babe," I said, "Try to give him something. He probably saved our lives."

Frank walked quickly out to try again to offer him something for his trouble. It had been only a matter of seconds, but the man was gone —driver and car were nowhere in sight!

The desk clerk was still marveling at how we had known about the room at that hour of the morning. Frank and I were first up to the desk. We were entitled to the room. Because it was 3:30 a.m., we offered to share the room with the soldier and his family. The room had two double beds, and they sent up a folding cot for Beau. That corner room at the Holiday Inn in St. Louis was a haven in a storm for two grateful families.

As I fell exhausted into bed, I asked Frank in a hushed whisper, "Could he have been an angel? How else would he have known we were there? How else would he have known where the only room was? Why wouldn't he take any money? How in the world could he have disappeared that fast?"

"That's a real question. I could see the highway from the front door of the Motel for miles in every direction. There was not a car in sight."

"Did you notice how that crazy blond guy wasn't afraid of you at all, but he was *terrified* of him?"

Frank heartily agreed. "He acted with authority, the way an angel would. Babe, one thing is sure, he was God's servant. When we go out in His name, His angels watch over us."

Chapter Twenty Two

Reflection

After our angel encounter, we decided that we would return to Brown's Cove, and spend some time in retreat, to review our commitment and our understanding of the Lord's call on our lives.

We knew the vision had called us to islands. But we'd seen other missions in our future, too.

Bill Beatty at Alleluia had given us the names and addresses of several priests in foreign countries who were engaged in the kind of evangelism and community building we were seeking. Frank wrote to them all during this time. We were confirmed in a growing sense of God's direction to Latin America.

We did a lot of praying, spiritual reading, and walking in the countryside, drawing very close together. Jim and Kathy enjoyed our fellowship, but we awaited a clear signal from the Lord indicating where He wanted us next.

It was my Dad's birthday, October 30th, 1976. John Finley invited us over for dinner, and we took the opportunity to use his telephone. The cottage in Brown's Cove didn't have one. After we exchanged birthday greetings, Mom got on the phone.

"Genie, I talked to Kay Listi a few days ago. She really wants you to call her. She and Vince have sold their home and they are going to build some kind of community where the old Our Lady of Lourdes church used to be."

"Really. Wow, Mom, that is so exciting. What else did she say?"

"I'm not so clear about everything. They're happy about it. I think she said that Vince quit his job and will be working at a Christian Service Center, or some kind of center, that Msgr. Mouton is starting," Mom answered.

"Quit his job? I can't believe it, I'm floored. Praise God!" I said enthusiastically.

By now, Beau and Frank's curiosity at the things they heard on my side of the conversation had gotten the better of them and they were bombarding me with questions. I asked Mom to hold a minute so I could relay the information. Then I got back to her.

"Frank wants to know who else is going to live in the community? Did she tell you?"

"Do you remember Judy? She used to be Judy Hebert, Daddy's secretary at the Vermilion Savings and Loan?"

"Yes, she and her husband, Red Bernard, were one of the couples that used to meet with us out at the farm before we left for the missions. They have a precious baby, Pamela," I responded.

"Kay told me they're going to be in the community, too. I understood that they wish y'all would come home and be in it," Mom said. I could tell she hoped we would do that.

I whispered to Frank, while holding my hand over the phone. "Red and Judy are doing it, too."

Frank looked so pleased. "Ask your Mom to call the Listis and tell them we'll be home as soon as possible."

"Mom, Frank wants me to ask you to call Kay and tell her we'll be home soon. Can you do that?" I asked.

"I'll call her tonight, that's good news to me. We'll be happy to have y'all around here for awhile," she said.

Later that evening, we returned to Jim and Kathy's cottage. During our family prayer time, Frank shared, "The community

Go! You Are Sent

thing in Abbeville is our clear signal. We can wait there to hear from our inquiry about serving in Colombia, and we can help them build the community."

"Maybe we can ride with Jim to Charlottesville tomorrow and book passage on the train to New Orleans." Beau said.

"Frank, remember that passage in the book of the prophet Habbakuk, about the vision? It looks like the Lord is fulfilling the vision. The Listis have prayed so hard about building a community," I commented.

"God is faithful to those who want to serve Him. Speaking about that passage. It's time to take stock of our life and vision. The passage says to 'Write the vision clearly on the tablets.' Why don't we write in our journal the things that God clarified for us during our last retreat?" Frank asked.

"Can you get the journal, please?" I asked Beau.

"Sure Mom, I'll hold Sarah while you write everything down," Beau said.

God *had* clarified our understanding of who we were. We would need His help daily to live out our call.

As we wrote these five essentials for our life, we asked God to write them on our hearts:

1. Proclaim the Gospel boldly.
2. Build Christian community.
3. Serve the poor.
4 Gospel poverty. Live a radical Gospel life,
   trusting the Lord to provide all our needs.
5. Live this life as faithful Catholics, with our
   worship centered in the Eucharist.

A few days later, we boarded the train that would take us back to Cajun country.

"I love this time of the year in Abbeville. I hope the Steen's syrup smell is still in the air," I thought. "Maybe a missionary community is starting there."

"Frank, God is in this turn of events. I don't know why, but He's sending us home. I'm really at peace about this," I shared later as we settled in on the train.

"A missionary is one who is sent. I'm confident that God's sending us home to encourage the Listis and the Bernards," Frank said.

"It's amazing. Four years ago, we didn't even know Jesus. I constantly thank Him for the way we've been able to go about as the Spirit blows," I said as the clickety-clack of the rails below rocked Sarah to sleep in my arms.

"The most important thing for a missionary to do is to Go," Frank said, and kissed baby Sarah on the cheek.

"He's right," I thought. "Go! Go without counting the cost. Go without questioning. Go in humble obedience. Go in His name so that others will believe that He lives. Go in the power of the Holy Spirit. Go to those who wait. Go in faith. Go armed for the battle. Go, conquer evil with good. Go with the Gospel to the ends of the earth!"

Epilogue

Saying, "Yes, Lord, we will go!" propelled us into an incredible odyssey of faith that took us in this story on our first missionary journey to Polynesia, the Navajos, the Mexican-American Border, the Alleluia Community, the hills of Virginia, and finally into the care of an angel in the St. Louis train station. God's angels continually kept a close watch over our lives, even in the farthest corners of the globe. Subsequent journeys took us to Mexico, Colombia, Canada, New Zealand, Australia, the Philippines, the Caribbean, and to the Diocese of the Caroline Islands in Micronesia. But that first journey was a formative one; the truths Jesus taught us then have been the foundation of our lives.

Jesus told us to "Go tell everyone." Everywhere we went, friends told us "You should write a book." God's miraculous intervention in our lives and ministry remained constant. In fact, more exciting chapters about two more missionary journeys are already written in rough draft form, and we trust there are more to come.

We experienced an epic, interior odyssey. "In season and out," Jesus called us to change, to become like Him.

God increased the numbers of His Summers rand of missionaries by sending us five more children after Sarah. Today our children are our greatest treasures and, by far, the best witnesses to the Lord's way. Once, on a three day silent retreat,

I heard God tell me, "Genie, you need to thank Me that you're privileged to live in such a Holy Company."

I do thank Him for their faith, purity, and hope. In his teenage years, Beau became a dynamic youth minister. His tremendous, unshakable faith inspires me. He has a master's degree in History from LSU. After starting out as an "only child," Beau has loved and cherished each of his siblings.

Susanna Maria was born in Colombia, in 1978. Susanna's sunny smile blesses everyone she meets. She was selected Lafayette's Junior Miss in 1994. After her selection as St. Thomas More High School's homecoming queen in 1994, she said, "Daddy, the whole school voted for Jesus, because that is what I represent." On our short mission to Micronesia, she graduated from Saramen Chuuk Academy. Susanna so easily says, "Yes, Lord, send me."

Mary Magdalen, born in Abbeville, in 1980, is the darling of our family. She radiates the strength of her faith and served in junior high as a cheerleader. Now, as a Honor Roll Sophomore at St. Thomas More, she shines for Jesus.

Simon-Peter was born on Christmas day, 1982, in Malaybalay, Bukidnon, Philippines. Simon is our special child, born with Prader-Wili Syndrome. My Dad says, "Simon's a genius at love." He loves Jesus, being an altar boy, Special Olympics, people in need, and any kind of pasta.

Joseph Anthony, was born in Manila, Philippines in 1984. We call him our strong man of God, a prayer warrior who stands tall for Jesus. Joseph inherited his dad's love for the great outdoors, and loves to hunt.

John Paul was born in Abbeville, in 1986. He regularly reads his Bible, enjoys praising the Lord, and shares with insight through the spiritual gift of visions. He is our family's best fisherman.

Each one of our children has his or her exciting mission stories to tell. They, too, have seen the powerful way God answers prayer. Jesus directs their lives in family prayer, daily private prayer, and in his gifts of the Holy Spirit.

From our earliest connection with the people of God, we've understood our need to be in community and fellowship with other committed Christians. Five years ago God raised up a group of families and young people to spend three Saturday nights a month in animated, exciting High Praise and Intercession. We share life, support each other's ministries, and are truly refreshed by a new wave of the Holy Spirit. As our numbers are multiplying, we affirm in our motto, "Our God is an Awesome God."

There's a tremendously touching story that I hope to tell one day, together with my son, Paul Nicholas Jordan. By the mighty hand of God, I have been reunited after thirty years with the baby I surrendered for adoption. He and my new daughter-in-law Patricia, and their children, Elise and Jameel, are a joy to me.

In this book, Sarah is the baby. She spent most of her young life in the missions, but graduated from St. Thomas More, where her prayers and witness had a transforming effect on the student body. She was named a National Merit Scholar. On May 28, 1994, she was wed to a strong, Christian man, Jason Spiehler. Jason's faith has had a real impact in his own family and on the Kingdom of God. As a married couple, their commitment to holiness at LSU is a sign of God in the midst of the academy. On June 22, Sarah and Jason presented Frank and me with our first Grandchild, Alyse Elizabeth Spiehler. Sarah will receive her degree in Spanish next year. Jason will graduate in psychology.

Spiritually, the wedding itself was the fruit of our life and mission. Jesus presided. The Holy Spirit was the principal Guest, and an aura of holiness filled the Church. Sarah and Jason truly became one in Christ. They asked Frank to sing a song he wrote in Brown's Cove when Sarah was a baby. It has been a theme song for our family life. When he sang, hearts were moved. As Sarah and Jason faced Frank, they accepted the song as a father's advice to his daughter and her groom on their wedding day:

"Walking with Jesus"
Walking with Jesus, living in the light,
Trusting in my Savior, day and night.
Walking in His Spirit, going where it blows,
Trusting in His graces, that's how a Christian grows.

Focus on this day, don't worry about the next.
Put on the yoke of Jesus, and give it your very best.
First love the Lord God, with all your might,
Then love your neighbor, you'll be walking in the light!

Speak out the good news, help those in need.
Have a servant's heart, and die to worldly greed.
Be kind and gentle, always do what's right.
In this world of darkness, you'll be holding up the light!

I'm walking with Jesus, living in His light,
Trusting in my Savior, day and night.
Walking in His Spirit, going where it blows,
Trusting in His graces, that's how this Christian grows!!

This is the song. It proclaims our faith. And because of that faith, we will always be happy to answer God's call. When He asks, "Whom shall I send?" we will say, "We will go, Lord. Send us."